FREE LOVE, FREE FALL

Scenes from the West Coast Sixties

by
Merimée Moffitt

Copyright 2016 by Merimée Moffitt

ABQ Press Trade Paperback Edition 2016

Cover design by George Paloheimo Jr.

Author portrait photograph by Georgia Santa Maria

Cover photograph by George H. Conger

www.abqpress.com
Albuquerque, New Mexico

ISBN 978-0-9966214-4-1

Also by Merimée Moffitt

Making Little Edens

This book is dedicated to the students who encouraged me to write my stories just as I encouraged them; to my supportive sister, Gretchen, who read my manuscripts and urged me forward; my poetry friends; my prose-writing friends; husbands and boyfriends; my kids whom I hope will continue to forgive me my shortcomings and defects; to both my brothers who at one time or another encouraged me to write more; and to those who were there but are here no more.

Preface	i
Introduction	1
Steve	7
Fun	19
Pea Harvest	43
Goose Hallow	57
Woolsey Street, Owsley, and LSD	65
Leaving Steve the First Time	77
The Red Dog Saloon	95
Dining in the Haight	105
Carol and the Dead	127
Hanging with the P. H. Phactor	139
Janis and Injustice for All	153
Diane	159
Fell Street on the Panhandle	169
Free Love, Free Fall	181
Isham	199
Hey Hippie, El Rito, NM, 1970	209
Michael	229
The Cabin	245
Learning to Speak Up, Out, and Over	259

Preface

When I was twelve or so, my mother had just had her fifth baby, money was tight, and there was only one bookshelf in our small house. The shelf, tucked into the low divider of a rental home in Eureka, California, separated dining room from living room and held what was left of the books my father had collected in high school and college. Prior to our stay in this house, there'd been several hasty moves brought on by bankruptcy, and I suspect that he'd lost more than a few of his precious possessions. One evening after dinner, on a rare note of familial content and adventure, my mother asked me to select something from the shelf to read to her and my father while they relaxed at the table with their coffee and smokes. My mother, a Stanford dropout for reasons that remain mysterious, was holding the newest addition to the family, and my little brothers must have been scrambling around nearby. I did as was asked and selected a book of poetry, opened randomly, and began to read.

After a few stanzas, which I recall enjoying although the meaning was lost on me entirely, my mother interrupted with amazement: "She reads beautifully, as if she knows what she's doing." I delighted in the praise, and secretly understood that I did know what I was doing. I was reading poetry—musical words written in lines of sound and image. Word puzzles. Over time, I was sure I'd learn more about what it all meant.

Earlier in my childhood, in a house farther south in California, my father had taken to reading *Ivanhoe* at bedtime to me and my sister with whom I shared a bedroom. I recall the sound of the sentences and his voice, and at that point, my father's love for books began its transfer to the next generation.

Books were the only toys we'd been allowed to take along on our two middle-of-the-night moves. Bankruptcy behavior in pre-computer days included nocturnal fleeings from creditors, but somehow, our set of *World Literature for Children* managed to survive as we headed north, each time, in the night. I used these books as blocks. I built doll castles out of them and adored the illustrations, but my father's adult books were my first introduction to reading literature.

A third uprooting and a move farther north to Eugene, Oregon, left me a displaced teen—a sassy California girl in the midst of teenaged Oregonians who hated little in life more than they hated California girls. That's when I really started with the inside of books, on my own. School became a do-able game, and at home, my only distraction from the tedium of housework, babies, and homework was my father's books.

Daddy, in his inimitable way, told me to go ahead and read them all. By this time his library covered a whole wall, floor-to-ceiling, and I started with the most accessible shelves. Some guidance might have been nice, but my parents weren't really the guiding type. Talking to teens wasn't even considered wise in 1959, as far as my parents knew, so in lieu of actual communication, my father made the notable suggestion of rewarding me with five dollars for every honest book report I could produce on books from his library. The move to Oregon paid off financially for my folks, so he could afford the price, and I could afford the time; reading and writing became a painless means of padding my pocketbook. The five dollars per pathetic report was nice, but most of all, I remember the few seconds of being in my father's presence as he opened his wallet and dished out the dough. Never receiving feedback on the reports, I became certain that he found reading and commenting on them beyond his dignity.

In all fairness, I was well into the books before the book report deal. I think the money was my father's way of showing an approval he never could bring himself to actually discuss. Did fathers in those days think they'd lose their virility if they conversed with children? Teachers, as some of you may recall, didn't exactly elicit conversations from teenagers then, either. Our world, in the early sixties, at least in Oregon, in the family I lived in, was a silent one. That is, until all hell broke loose.

Some of the titles and authors of Daddy's books were ones that I used as starters. If I liked them, I'd get to the library and find more by the same author. Hence, Steinbeck's body of work and Doris Lessing's, likewise Simon de Beauvoir, Alberto Moravia (who, mixed with rural Catholicism put quite a twist on my concept of sex), Stendhal, Kerouac, Daphne du Maurier, Camus, Voltaire (Daddy went to U. of Santa Clara and Berkeley), Willa Cather, Kafka. Of course, once I'd started messing around looking for books in the library, I found the Russians and authors of trashy historical fiction (early romance genre?) whose names are long lost to me, but whose images of ravishing and ravished heroines remain vivid.

An old-lady English teacher, maybe my senior-year teacher, wrote in the margin of my journal once, that I was "verbally very deft." I was acutely aware from this comment that verbal deftness was a minor achievement, but it was recognition. I longed to be praised for charm or powers of observation, or cleverness—but "verbally deft" was the prize I took with me on my vagabond travels.

Within months of graduating in the top ten (out of four hundred or so) in 1963, I was in Portland, at Reed College, learning how to be a beatnik, my sole reason for selecting Reed. By that time, Dylan, Baez, Herman Hesse, the Beatles and the Beats were causing me an itching curiosity about alternate life-styles.

It was at Reed where I fell apart. Studying ten hours a day and feeling abandoned by my family, I stopped eating and took up with Reed's night-watchman, an upper-classman from Portland State (whose wife was a Reedie) who was willing to work with me on my virginity problem. This young man also introduced me to the "Portland scene" –musicians, poets, dreamers, and their hangers-on who partied and hiked the hills and smoked marijuana and interacted and talked. Beatniks!

I tossed out school, education, books and the straight life I'd been leading. I wanted to be bold; I wanted to find a way to get free of the grip that society had on women (me). I dropped out (pre-Timothy Leary), turned on, and proceeded to live my life as it happened. *Free Love. . .* is an attempt to look back and find out what happened and why.

My family disowned me, literally typed up and co-signed by the two of them. My mother's anger and horror at my outlandish styles and refusal to get back on track at her command gave me my freedom, more than I wanted at times. I remained as attached as possible to my older sister Gretchen (Gigi) who advised me once that life was something you lived, not a set of rules, not a future—be here now was what she meant. My younger brother Charlie was my anchor, the one person in my family who steadfastly treated me with kindness and respect. He sent me empty journals that I filled, always thinking they'd be a reference for the real thing some day, a book. By the time I'd succumbed to therapy, in my late twenties as a single mom of a four-year-old son, the journals represented the former, depressed me, and I impulsively threw them into a dumpster, all fifteen or twenty of them. They had covered about two feet of shelf space. After a year or two, I did regret the tossing of the journals (I may have misinterpreted my therapist's advice to clean up all my old business and get over the past), but the symbolic act was matched by a positive change in my life. *Free Love* is a revisiting of what might have been notated in the journals.

Day by day, man by man, from growing up and learning the hard way, from a PhD in the school of hard knocks, through therapy, Sufi dancing, meditation, and self-awareness trainings and finally a child, I steered myself back to what I had been good at: school, reading, writing, housework, children.

Before actually returning to college, I had started taking writing workshops wherever I could find them. My first was in Taos on Natalie Goldberg's living room floor. Well, it was a two-room adobe, and we gathered on her rug once a week and wrote, drank tea, smoked, read and laughed together. Natalie charged five dollars (either per night or for the whole set of nights) I can't remember, and on an open-door basis, a few faithful women showed up regularly. Natalie, shortly thereafter, abandoned us for greener pastures in Colorado. Some of us gathered again in a group at the Mabel Dodge Lujan House with a woman who was renting it at the time. One more session of lessons followed with a local journalist named Jim, and the series of home-style lessons eventually led to returning to college, first at New Mexico State branch campus in Alamogordo. I returned with hopes of writing. I finished my degree in Liberal Arts with dozens of hours in writing workshops and secondary certification in the areas of English and math (one of my many deviations). I transferred to UNM, remarried and had two more children. Financial pressures then necessitated an exit from academia as soon as possible, so I chose teaching. In the work world, I wanted something that would be working with teenagers. In teaching writing to teens, the issue of following one's dreams is a recurring theme, and so *Free Love* is a "put my money where my mouth is" result of practicing what I preach. Teenagers can smell a fake a mile away, and my students have been instrumental in my determination to get something together, to write something, to graduate, to publish.

My first job in teaching was with gifted eighth graders called Enriched Language Arts, a job I walked into, thank goodness, due to all those hours in Creative Writing. One of my students in our classroom writing-workshop setting, said, "Gee, Mrs. Moffitt, it must have been so much fun to grow up in the sixties." That comment called for a response, in writing, hence, my book. Other students, over my years of teaching writing within the English curriculum, have been very encouraging. What was it like? What happened? One kid told me he liked my writing so much, he'd read anything I wrote. (I often taught writing by participating and sharing with the students.) He promised me that I couldn't go wrong. And eventually, I started in earnest. Out of the mouths of babes, and they're waiting. They're waiting for my book. Of course, they're older now as am I.

My process has been to look back at my adventures, my Kerouac-influenced activities: hitch-hiking, partying, happening to be in the happening places, drugs, sex, and rock 'n roll as it unfolded around me. I look at crazy parent things, my siblings from the same weird pod and period, my pre-gay-lib brother and my repressed-artist sister, all of us engaged in struggles to survive and thrive in the same time frame. I've always wanted to somehow trace the insanity of our Irish alcoholic parents through the things we did and suffered, through struggling to live honestly, truly, successfully, and with love.

The ensuing set of stories has come out of my desire to capture a piece of how it really was, what it was like to be there, in the sixties, as me: a child of the times; of parents who loved but not adequately, not soberly; amidst protestors and some women with voices as I tagged along with crazy men, unaware of my own voice, unconsciously struggling to find one. Not until the first issue of *Ms.* magazine did I realize I was not alone in the world. At that point, reading that magazine, sitting in my own two-room adobe—well, not mine, I wasn't together enough to own property or call anything my own—in that little rental cabin, I began to realize I existed. Gloria Steinem and her writers were speaking to me, to us, writing that we, too, could have a say in things, and that we should speak.

In the long and short of it, I love to read and to hear other peoples' stories, and I have attempted to contribute to the body of work on our beautiful planet. In classrooms, I have encouraged students to express opinions and to realize that they are in charge of their own lives. I tell them to believe in their own stories and that their own stories are worthy material for poems and fiction and essays. Those who do write, those who do speak out and up, cannot know what influence they may have, cannot decide in advance what comfort or hope, solace or inspiration they may give. I tell my students that they'll never know unless they try, unless they commit that physical act of getting the words on the page. *Free Love* is meant to entertain and possibly to inform, but most of all, *Free Love* is my speaking out, my finding of my voice (albeit better late than never), my living up to my own ideals and beliefs.

Introduction: Dropping Out of Reed College, 1964

You realize you are about to leave the beaten path; all the girls you met at school are doing better than you, well maybe your mural-painting friend was failing too—you don't really know—failing as in running out of steam, juice, caring. The deans had said murals on dorm walls were no longer allowed. You and she had been caught hitch-hiking to Seattle at night in the rain. You were caught shoplifting a pack of gum. The dean of women had said "Amoral" to your atheist father, regarding your attitude. Your father calls and asks what the hell is going on, and you say you don't like college, you hate it actually. That choice was made in your math class when the x's and y's and a's and b's didn't matter of a sudden, not in any way; you no longer wanted to play with unknowns in equations. You thought maybe you would never care again about math problems with equations and unknowns. There were more interesting non-knowns than symbols scribbled in chalk by droning men in a classroom. You wanted three-dimensional play things, thick-chested men, rides in cars, picnics. That was it. You wanted your life to be a picnic, not blackboards covered with letters and numerals.

Picnics were the thing your mother did for fun, with all the kids and a green river just right for swimming. In Humanities, you didn't care either, about Plato's cave or anything they asked you to read. You'd read all the books on your father's shelves that you could reach, mostly the good story-tellers like Steinbeck, Kerouac, de Beauvoir, Stendhal, Cather. It was cold in the lecture hall with the old church pews, where a dull person lectured about ideas you didn't understand or love, at 9am every rainy morning.

You don't love anything except food and food is forbidden, so you eat ice cream sandwiches from the basement machine. You had self-forbidden food when a boy from South Eugene sent a message that you were fat, too fat to date. That boy's words corroborated your mother's. She'd told you when you were little, "No men will love you if you're fat." But you were nine then. You didn't like men at age nine, but at fifteen you thought you deserved a good-looking guy adoring you, walking at your side, your interests ought to be of importance to him, and you didn't think you were too fat. But no, he said you were, and he dated a skinny friend of yours. You stopped eating breakfast and most lunches. You got thin and enjoyed being thin, and you went away to Reed to find Beatniks who might be interesting. And here you are. You'd read *On the Road*. You'd been reading everything you could find since the move from

California to Eugene when you were a sophomore, when you found out Oregon girls hated everyone from California, especially you and your sister.

You stopped leaving the dorm building, stopped going to classes or the dining hall, stopped walking around campus. You drove your roommate's car in the rain a few times, to nowhere, or to Rose's Deli to get a forbidden cinnamon roll or chocolate cake, and you hated yourself for wanting sweets and feeling too full when you had barely eaten a thing, but of course you were starving. You stopped playing your guitar or thinking that you were pretty and smart enough. No one seemed to care.

Your father suggests you leave college if you dislike it so much. He has never suggested anything to you before. He had invited you and your sister to a French movie once, *Jules and Jim*, and you were impressed that she, the Jeanne Moreau character, had two lovers. You wanted a lover but you were alone all the time at Reed, at seventeen, and it never stopped raining. Never.

The day your father comes to get you, your dorm mates have a little goodbye party in your dorm room as a surprise. You smile, genuinely touched that they care when you had barely known them, barely hung out, hardly spoken. They give little gifts and cards and there is a cake. No one has ever been quite so kind like that. It's as if a light turns on for a few minutes and you can see the possibilities of surprise, unselfish kindness. You had been so quiet, but they care that you lost your balance, your momentum. They were so relieved it was you and not them leaving, leaving too early like an aborted fetus. Maybe they knew why they were there, when you had no clue. What did they know? They wished you all the luck, fifty years ago now. As your father drives you away from the campus you feel as if you had unplugged yourself from any plan you ever had.

But you had met some Beatniks, and one of them would follow you; he would find you and you would be partners on the road, the wandering, meandering path, for several years. You didn't know that yet, but he would call your mother in Eugene, and she would give him, long-haired and insanely handsome, your phone number at your cousin's apartment in San Francisco. Did she want you to take up with this voice on the phone? Was she glad that a man actually wanted you? You met him the night the dorm mother at Reed had called to you from the foot of the stairwell: "Merimée, you have a gentleman caller," and there was Steve at the big oak door, grinning, soaking wet in the early evening rain. You didn't know him, so he had some explaining to do. She allowed you to invite him into the sitting room.

"LP sent me," he had said, grinning. LP was the boring beatnik who'd taken you through Reed College's canyon (now known as the Reed wetlands), naming and pontificating on every genus. "He said I ought to meet you." This long-haired, blonde Steve who had just arrived from Seattle emphasized everything with his earnest smile and sort of manly demeanor. He was older, eight years older than you, and rugged with a workingman's body and bright blue eyes. You had invited him into the room where girls were allowed to entertain. As soon as the housemother was gone, you told him to follow you up to your second-floor garret room, which might have been a fun place had you been conscious enough to understand fun. But you were so young, so inexperienced. Good grades yes, but mostly, you'd worked for your mom, cleaning her house, feeding her babies, babysitting the toddler—going to your room and staying quiet. Not much preparation for leaving home, but along with a few sewing and cooking lessons, it was all you had besides your honor student status and a healthy appetite for your parents' alcohol.

Sitting in the one chair, in the same room where you would learn that Kennedy had been shot and killed—the room where you had been looking out on day rain, night rain, and afternoon drizzle for endless weeks—you and he talked into the night. He was decidedly odd, and not a boy. You'd never dealt with anyone already married and divorced, already in and out of the Army. What was he doing in your dorm room? You weren't instantly wild about him. He sat on the floor cross-legged even when your roommate came in and slept—no interruption in your sober, comfortable conversation. But somehow this man and you clicked; you had no idea he'd take the initiative eventually and you would share a four-year path. That first night, you talked and laughed. You make one run out for a second pack of Camels just before midnight curfew; in those days, the dorms had cigarette machines in the basement.

When he finds you in the City, San Francisco, a couple months later, you decide he'd do just fine as a rescue prince. You would follow him like you were a lost puppy, and it was all meant to be. You can smile about those days now.

Merimée Moffitt

Steve

I had signed up for Reed looking for Kerouac's beatniks, but missed them, really, by a couple of years. When I dropped out it was pre-hippie time, and I was caught in between.

Just after winter break, I returned home and my parents said school or job. I found myself working at the phone company in San Francisco, Ma Bell it was called then, where I also felt out of place (no interest in pretty nails and high heels); then Steve showed up at my cousin's apartment, where my sister and I were crashing until further notice (our own basement apartment having proven untenable).

The weekend Steve showed up, my cousin had been trying to teach me how to be bulimic, but I was failing. I could only burp, no matter what I ate or gorged on or drank; not even soapy water would make me barf. I was failing at everything: staying thin, college, having an apartment, having one half of an idea of who I was and why I was in a stupid job in the city.

When I opened the door to Steve this time, he looked like my first good meal in ages. I was Cinderella and he was, having let his hair grow, a handsome prince with my glass slipper in hand, my ride away, my path different.

"You wanna go for a ride," he said, grinning, when I opened the door of my cousin's apartment.

"How did you find me?" I was so happy to see him, so delighted that I was going to be allowed some reprieve from total confusion. I think I imprinted on him right then, as if I were a tiny chick he'd watched until I hatched.

"Your mother," he said. "I called and she gave me your number and address." I was glad she didn't mind just handing me over to him. "I'm going over to Mount Tamalpais for a hike. Wanna come?" Still grinning, but he had a pretty smile. I would have gone anywhere with him.

"I'll get my jacket," I said and by that time my sister and cousin were at the door saying hello to him, and I hoped my sister was good and jealous, or at least impressed that I could drum up a date like Steve.

It was a miracle to me that he had followed me and found me again, and this time not only did I have good use for him, but also he was looking extravagantly sexy in an old, dark-brown bomber jacket (genuine World War II) with a borrowed BMW motorcycle ready to take me across the bay to Mount Tam. I did consider that the bike was "borrowed," but it was a getaway, and I chose not to be too fussy about the details. I grabbed my jacket, put on shoes, and we were off. I suspected it would be several years we'd spend together and it was—four, just about exactly—and he did turn out to be a landmark on the trail to my own voice, self-awareness, responsibility, and my raison d'être.

It was so long cousin, so long Ma Bell, so long to my brief solitude. I may as well have been jumping through some primitive marriage hoop when I jumped on the back of his bike and slipped my arms around his perfect waist, his shoulders broad enough to carry a wood-burning cook stove down a mountain. I watched him do that, later, when we spent a winter in Seattle.

It was possibly the happiest wedding day of all the times I would commit some part or all of myself to a man—just a date to go hiking, really, but I knew it was more. He had not only come looking for me a second time, but he had become attractive, long-legged in blue jeans, with rolled-up sleeves on his chambray shirt, boots, that bomber with the sheepskin collar catching his leonine mane, and he was happy. He smiled and was so glad to see me, too. We liked each other, my prince and I. He had a plan, and blue eyes the color of a stormy sea, and I would be his girl.

It was that kind of day as we crossed the Golden Gate, with a sunny sky and twinkling sea, the arches orange and gleaming. Mt. Tam was new to me, and I was enthusiastic about the hike. Perfect spring weather with a touch of fall still lingering on the almost season-less trail, some golden leaves yet to rot, some green ones rising to the call of the sun, the main path packed with mulch to silence everything—the quiet of a mountain in dappled light. We walked forever and then a lake appeared. Steve asked if I'd like to swim across. It was February, and I didn't think outdoor swimming was wise; it just didn't fit into my version of enjoyable swimming.

He then treated me to a full view of a body he seemed not the least bit embarrassed to uncover, and he looked divine. I stood behind him on the leaf-packed trail as he stripped; I was somewhat astonished since my only sexual activities hadn't had the benefit of daylight. From behind, he was Adonis executing a lovely flat dive and swimming like crazy across and back; as he shook the water off like a puppy, all golden-haired and tan as he was, I averted my eyes. He dressed. We moved on. He laughed about everything, and I was definitely falling under his magic spell.

Eventually fatigue set in and I asked about turning around; was there a plan? We were in a clearing, facing what looked like a mountain to me, and he said his friends lived just over the next hill, that we'd go see if they were home then catch a ride back to the bike. He estimated ten miles as the distance we'd cover altogether. I sucked it up and pretended I wasn't dying of thirst and hunger. Thank God his charming friends in the little wooden cottage with a deck on the side of the hill were home, and that the woman of the house had a cauldron of soup and chunks of homemade bread for us—more magic in fairy land. We stood in her kitchen chowing down, sipped a couple glasses of wine, and the mister took us in his truck back around the base of the mountain to the motorcycle. Steve took me home as the sun was setting—was it all orchestrated to knock my socks and the rest of my clothing off? Quite likely, and the plan eventually worked. But I was dropped at my cousin's that night and I slept alone.

He called me the next day about going to a little club in Oakland to see a cool musician named Chuck Berry.

Steve guessed I'd like this guy's stuff, based on my obsession with the Beatles and my readiness to defend rock 'n' roll as a valid musical form. And yes, of course, it was fabulous. Chuck Berry was strutting and singing his soon-to-be-hits in an almost-empty club. I was thrilled. Back in the pickup Steve had borrowed from Earl, the owner of the motorcycle too, we had a jug of wine at our feet; my sister and Earl were in the camper behind us, and we passed the jug around, singing silly folk songs Steve was teaching us. "Ain't It Grand To Be a Christian?" was my favorite, and we'd sing it all across the country a few days later when Gretchen and I ditched our jobs and our sofa space at the cousin's, and were off to New York City to drop off Earl at the Great Lakes and ourselves in a friend's apartment while we found work and a place to live. A plan—it turned out Steve always had a plan. Usually fairly short term, but at least a plan.

That night the jug of wine and singing and high spirits of the evening loosened me up—surely not the best way for Steve to have gotten into my pants but possibly the only way at the time. I had a long road ahead of me, on which sex and booze and drugs were inextricably linked. He took all four of us to a "friend's house" for which he had a key—it was obviously a woman's place, a little nook of an apartment on Potrero Hill, one room with a loft, so artsy I was in love with it right away. Gretchen and I went into the bathroom, and as she peed and I washed up a bit, she asked me, "Have you and Steve done it yet?" And I looked at her, sort of surprised, as she and I had been together like 24/7 until she and Earl were in the back of the truck in the camper.

"No," I said, looking at her and realizing she was about to tell me that she and Earl had. I was a bit shocked, but then again, she was older and had experience. It was her first date with the guy. I guessed that to borrow Earl's pickup, Steve had set up the double date and it all seemed a good idea, but sex already? My family was pretty much without a moral compass, but they took a lot of stock in competition. We all knew my dad had been maxima cum laude, my mom on a merit scholarship. A lot of good that did her, dropping out of Stanford after the first year because no sorority accepted her? Poor mom. But that night, I figured I'd best not let my sister have one up on me and, already so drunk I could barely negotiate the ladder to the big two-bed loft where Steve had told me to go wait for him, I decided I too would "do it"—my sister had always been the star I followed ever since birth, when my mother set me down and told me to tag along with her, do what she did, go where she went. We were Irish twins just eighteen months apart.

Earl was the next one up the ladder and when he saw me lying naked in a drunken stupor, he did what a lot of guys might have done and I didn't care. I was too drunk to consider anything but skin on skin and being silly and bad—I was interested in what really constituted the "bad" that the nuns had served up as worthy of eternal damnation in a hellfire of immortally burning briquettes. It didn't seem to me that letting Earl have a go at me was worthy of any God-on-high attention—who would care which guy it was ravishing me? A not-so-wise seventeen-year-old? Steve told me in our later years that he remembered that event clear as a bell and had considered killing Earl, but decided to let it all go. He told Earl to get away. Steve may have been claiming me, but I had shown, as clearly as I could show him, that no man was going to own me. I would play by my own rules, especially if playing with the big boys. I wasn't looking for an owner, just a pal. A friend, really, and Steve was seriously amusing and wild enough to be full of surprises and thrills. I imagined that we were having fun. The devil be damned; I was my own person and my own body and having two men in one night was intriguing.

I, as the good daughter I was, wrote my parents a note letting them know that their daughters, Gretchen and I, would be leaving the city and heading east to the other city, the Big Apple, with a couple of guys we'd met, and I gave them my new boyfriend's name and a false one at that. (Earl was a merchant marine with papers and would be storing his vehicles with friends while he went back to work his stint on the Great Lakes.) The little lie about Steve's name did represent a turning in the road, though not in the lying to my parents, which I'd been doing for years in the normal teenage way of protecting my mother from unnecessary upsets. So many times when I spoke the truth, she'd come unhinged, to the point of kicking or slapping me—lying was so much more pleasant. Why would she really care if I were driving around chasing boys up and down Main Street instead of studying at the library? I did my studying. There was nothing fun at home except eating, and honestly, flirting with boys is a natural invitation to lie. The intuitive decision to give a false name to my new boyfriend and traveling companion was key to my remaining with him. I just sensed it.

When our parents found out from me that we were crossing the state line with two men, my mother, without even attempting to reach me via house phone, decided to call the police and have me arrested so she would be able to speak to me before I left the world as she knew it. However, the day before she alerted the San Francisco juvenile detention squad that her daughter was about to become a runaway with an older man, Steve and I had spent the evening at LP's younger brother's house in Berkeley. This man was a meth cook and dealer who worked for Sierra Designs as an inventor—specifically, of a down stuffing machine that put Sierra in the lead for the new down-jacket craze. His meth was something entirely new to me, but I was childlike enough to do as I was told. I was in no way able to judge for myself without at least trying something out. And so I tried the meth, and too much of it at once. These self-appointed self-medicators who shot me up, damn near split my head open. It was a painful overdose, which likely did damage and surely made me crazy and paranoid, fearful and sort of brain-dead for the duration—who'd want that?

The bruises on my inner arms from being done up by incompetents were glaring when we arrived back at my cousin's apartment at dawn the next morning. Two plainclothesmen jumped out of a car; one grabbed me, and the other flung Steve across the hood of their innocuous sedan. They asked him for his name and ID, and this is where the little lie changed my life. He gave his name, and they let him go. "Not the guy we're looking for," one said, and then asked Steve if he knew a Robert Evans, and of course he said no. But my own name matched their paperwork, and I was rudely shoved into the backseat of their cop car. One of the detectives climbed in next to me. While en route to the juvenile detention center, he kept swinging his big set of keys against my thigh. I wasn't about to take the bait and fight with him. He probably wanted an altercation so he could justify "subduing" me, but I simply asked him to stop with the keys. He wouldn't tell me why I'd been picked up.

Getting booked at the D-home in San Francisco didn't bother me too much, especially since I was quick at saying yes when the matron with the clipboard asked if I had any contagious diseases. I was given a cell in solitary, feeling some gratitude for the so-called intelligence my parents had passed on to me and very lucky that I just happened to know the word "impetigo"; maybe there'd been an outbreak at Reed, but somehow I knew the name of a disease that pushed their buttons and got me a room of my own. The entryway into the jail had been straight out of a bad B movie. Girls holding the bars with two fists screaming "Bitch" or "White bitch" had warned me that I wasn't in the sunny flowerbeds of Oz, but more like mashed under a falling house into some dark perdition, and it was scary. I didn't want to be in the same quarters as those girls. The trick succeeded a bit too well as the tin box I was locked into became my home for two nights and three days. The afternoon of day three, after a raging and screaming fit of my own, partially induced by coming down off the voluminous amount of speed, I was relieved to see my mother in her proper bouffant, with her little handbag clutched tightly to her chest.

She took me to her brother's (my uncle's) office/apartment in North Beach, not some funky artist pad but two full floors of an iconic high-rise sitting right behind Coit Tower. But I didn't give a hoot about where we were. My uncle brushed me off with a cold hello—so much for those fun times he'd treated me to as a little kid. It wasn't as if my parents hadn't taken me to the bus stop themselves in Eugene with one hundred bucks and a suitcase and waved goodbye and good luck! I was doing the best I could. I'd found some fun friends and was *On the Road* à la Kerouac, my literary hero, headed east to New York City.

Mad at her for idiotically having me arrested when she could have just called to talk, I was still interested in what she had to say. We'd never done much talking other than her barking out my orders of the afternoon; she was my afterschool sergeant. That night, against the backdrop of a wall of glass looking out over the lights of San Francisco, my mother whined a bit about how she didn't really love my father, so how could she advise me, and that was that. So much for parenting. She could have lured me home but she did not—didn't want to, or didn't try. I was disappointed with her self-pity, but I had a life to lead, and she was no help to me, as far as I could see. I got dropped back at my cousin's apartment with no kiss from her for good luck, no wish for me to have a good life. As I let myself in, I noticed the now bigger blooming bruises inside both my arms where I'd been poked by the shared needle. Somehow, all the older adults so set on "helping me" hadn't even noticed.

The fact that my mother had let me sit in a jail cell for three days and two nights, and had put me there herself, wasn't so shocking to me then. It is poignant that my father didn't even come with her. Did they have any idea what the San Francisco detention center for girls was like? Why had she not even attempted to call me on the black dial-up at my cousin's apartment? I would have talked gladly. If she'd been concerned about me, she might have explained why and taken me back home. But none of that was how it was. She was performing some kind of hapless duty, turning over a fake rock that she knew had nothing under it—she didn't even know me, or care to. That was how I felt about her, my only mother. She loved her five o'clock drinks; she may have loved her three younger kids, the two boys and the baby girl. I admit they were darling. But my sister and I were dismissed, tossed and re-tossed into the night without much direction or encouragement, no guidance or ideas for how we might survive in the world. I could make a meatloaf and bake a cake, change diapers, feed babies, and wash floors. I was good at school, or had been, and my sister could type. I had refused to learn to type as I knew the typing pool was not a place I'd ever want to be. Books had given me ideas, and I was willing to trust the universe that I could, somehow, be part of a world where I did not get hit for speaking, put down for being female, told I'd never be loved if I ate enough to not be hungry. The same negativity was sending the boys to a trumped-up fake war. Somehow, I knew the war was macho bravado and BS. I wanted no part of anything resembling my parents' loveless marriage or dead-end jobs for women where pretty fingernails and spike-heeled shoes counted for more than brains. In hindsight, I can see that her lack of confidence left me motherless. I didn't know where the exit was, but a drive across the country with Steve and Earl seemed like a start on the unnamed path.

Eventually, and before her death thirty some years later, I would count up all the delicious meals she served us and forgive her for not being a magical mother who could have saved me from all the trouble I ran into. One therapist was quite certain it was her adversity that had made me so strong. I can buy that.

Steve had arranged for a drive-away car all the way to New York City and a friend's apartment. The next morning, with Earl and Gretchen in back, me in the front, and Steve driving—I think he drove the whole way—we were off on our grand adventure.

Fun

By mid-May, 1964, New York City was getting so hot we had taken to going naked half the day, only getting dressed to wander around the neighborhoods and parks in the late afternoon. We'd run out of Earl's dough and our own long since, and Gretchen wasn't going to want us hanging on, waiting for her to buy groceries. "We have to do something," I mumbled to Steve in bed one morning, hours after Gretchen had gone off to work. She, with her secretarial skills, had landed a job managing the maids in a big hotel—not bad.

"Yeah, I know. But I hate this city," he said. "There's nothin' here for me." He wanted to get back to the West Coast and fresh air. We'd dropped Earl at the Great Lakes to do his merchant-marine thing, but Steve hadn't gotten on without a union card. We were lying on white sheets in the sun that streamed through the only window in the tiny apartment bedroom. Yesterday's *Times* was spread around like a quilt; there was nothing that either of us wanted to do or were willing to do in the classifieds, and I was tired of reading, tired of my malaise. I didn't see our shared fifth-floor walk-up on Canal Street as something romantic and full of potential, or the city as one that was bursting with art and promise; I could only see him. I knew we were mooching off my sister, who was kindly sleeping on the sofa while we took the bedroom. My job in an art-making kiosk at the World's Fair was so thick and sticky with malaise I had left at the end of the first day and not gone back. I had no energy. Something was wrong.

"Well, what happens if we do go back to Oregon?" I asked. I knew we had to get jobs, and the trip across the country sounded fun, even if we didn't have money for tickets.

"I've driven dump trucks for the factory for years, so I know I can get on." Steve's eyes lit up as the plan formulated. He seemed excited. "You could get on in the factory working on the belt or stacking boxes or something," he said. "We just have to get there by June first to get on the list." I agreed as soon as I felt his enthusiasm, but that feeling of following a drug-taking farm boy washed through me. I was ever-so-vaguely aware that in choosing to follow this man, I would be getting some surprises that might not seem like first choices. With all of New York City in front of us, he wanted to run back West to where his comfort zone was, his old job, his life as a laborer and taxi driver, a dropout, and a drug taker. I had become attached to him; there was no independent thinking about myself. It was an "us" decision, or a "he" decision. No way could I fathom a future for myself—that would be in years to come—but I wanted to see and know this rural life too.

We agreed to hitch back to Oregon for the pea harvest in Weston, just across the border from Walla Walla, Washington. It was one week before the deadline of June 1. Gretchen didn't want to go, even though I encouraged her; she said she'd stay on in her good job managing the maid brigade to see what it would be like, sticking it out in New York all on her own. She thought Steve and I were both plumb nuts, going around naked and not finding work, wanting to hitch to Oregon when we'd only been in New York a couple months, but she did loan us sixty-five bucks for the trip across Canada. We'd decided on Canada because we guessed there'd be a direct highway all the way across. Maybe Steve felt less intimidated by Mounties than cops who might get him on a statutory charge. In those days it was illegal for an adult male to be shacking up with, especially crossing state lines, if not legally married, with an underage female. This way, we could also go through upstate New York, which was supposed to be beautiful.

We took the subway as far as it would go, and the plan then was to ride our thumbs all the way. I'd never hitchhiked, but the word itself was exciting to me because of Kerouac. I'd found *On the Road* in my dad's bookshelf, one of the many books he'd paid me to write a book report on. I had been deeply impressed with the idea of The Road—that life was literally and figuratively a Road, a Path, and that we ought to live it fully and joyously. That, at least, was a plan. In all my father's books, I may have been looking for a blueprint, some guidelines about how the heck to proceed. College had been an unspoken given from my dad's point of view, but he had never taken the time to talk to me, to ask even once about my interests while I was in high school, to somehow be one parent who was proposing something for me to set my sights on; I was clueless, too. But out of the books, came clues. I was without a rudder until Kerouac's joy, joy on the road, joy in relationships, fun, moving, exploring, getting one's mind blown by looking at a mountain, something wonderful . . . of course, he too ran into the realities of our limitations as humans. Before one can confront the wall, any wall, one must travel to it. I was eager to get out and move around, so it was so long New York City.

Before we left, Steve took me to the studio of Abby Shawn, Ben Shawn's daughter. Even I had heard of Ben Shawn, and this woman, Shawn's daughter, who lived in her studio was one of Steve's gazillion women friends. We also attended an evening soiree at the home of Rudy Wurlitzer Jr., heir to the Wurlitzer jukebox fortune. How Steve knew these people was beyond me, but I was enchanted, and Steve was often the provider of this form of entertainment. A couple of days later, we took the subway as far north as it went, and hit the road.

The first truck that picked us up dropped us somewhere upstate at twilight. Twilight, the time for mosquitoes, but I didn't know much about that. The driver just stopped his semi on the side of the road and said he'd be turning soon. "Well, thanks," I'd said, looking around at open country.

"Yeah, thanks, man," Steve added, as we backed down from the cab. We were a little puzzled as the guy roared off, wondering why he'd dump us between nothing and nowhere on a long stretch of country road. At first I thought there were leaves flying in the breeze or something because the particles hitting my face and arms and bare feet were so dense, but the air was still, and we weren't under trees. Tall grasses and what appeared to be a stream off to the side of the fields gave a lovely view, and I wondered if we should just stay for the night and start hitching again at dawn; then I realized what the flying objects were—mosquitoes the size of bumblebees—whapping at us as if competing to get the blood before their cousins or other relatives drained us dry.

"Steve!" I yelled at him as he was coming back from the bushes where he'd taken a pee. "I'm getting eaten alive." We both were slapping skin as fast as we could but not fast enough to keep up with the feast the little bugs were enjoying. It was a late spring dusk, the air was so thick with voracious bloodsuckers I was afraid, and there was not a vehicle in sight—a real trucker's joke.

"We better start running," Steve said, already turning back at me from a trot. "Let's keep moving and you stick out your thumb. I'll carry the pack and the sleeping bag." I'd been one of the slowest runners in every PE class of my life. As I started panting along behind Steve, who looked like he could gallop all the way to Oregon, I wondered if the trucker was laughing at us now. Steve had long, thick, golden hair that swept his shoulders, a style that just made a lot of straight, working types really mad. Being twenty-five years old, not working, hanging out with a teenage girl, and having the Thor-hair made him a target in '64. In 1964 it was a punishable crime for a guy to flaunt his lack of regard for society with the wrong-length hair, but the punishment was usually vigilante-style. The trucker had nailed us.

"Shit," I started screaming as I whapped bugs, my left thumb joggling along, sticking out into the road, but it was working. There were only about a dozen little suckers on me instead of hundreds. I was in a short, loose dress so they were all over my legs, too, but God and all her universe proved essentially good, and before I collapsed, a pickup pulled over in front of us. We threw our things in back and hopped into the front seat. It had only been a few minutes, but I knew I couldn't have lasted much longer.

He was an older guy; he said he'd be driving all night and most of the next morning, too, and he needed company to keep him awake. "Where you kids from?" His voice seemed friendly with just a bit of a Canadian accent; he was a nice man in a clean plaid shirt with a stubbly beard, maybe a day's worth. He wore a baseball cap and laced-up leather boots that looked comfortable. My sandals had broken the day before, leaving the city, and I'd tossed them—no money for shoes but it didn't matter. Hitching across Canada barefoot would be even more fun, I figured—different, and a statement about how much stuff we really don't exactly need. The driver of the truck made no remarks about our apparel or hair.

"We're from Oregon," I answered, sitting in the middle between the two men, "but we've been in New York a few weeks, visiting my sister." Steve had his arm on the back of the seat, loosely resting on my shoulders. I noticed how I didn't really want to tell the truth about myself, that I'd been doing nothing for weeks but screwing Steve all day every day and living off his friend's loan, and then my sister's first couple of paychecks. It wasn't so much to be telling someone about.

"Well, where're you headed now?" the guy asked.

"Oh, we're going back to Oregon," I said, "to work in the pea harvest. We have to get there by the first of June to get jobs." I thought about the list Steve said we'd have to get on, and I pictured the clipboard with our names. I'd have to use his last name, I realized, without being married. It would be odd to just take his name like that—no wedding, no proposal, just a silent capitulation. I had simply become his after our fourth date, by dint of necessity. I wondered how this really felt to me—to be his pretend wife—this cave-in to social norms I disagreed with in so many ways. But if we wanted to work, I knew it would have to be done. I couldn't be his whore and expect fair treatment, not way out in the country at least.

On our first date in San Francisco, Steve had ridden up on a borrowed motorcycle and taken me to Mount Tamalpais for a ten-mile hike on a beautiful day, then home across the Golden Gate Bridge under stars and the afterglow of the sunset. He'd taken me to meet some friends of his where they listened to jazz and drank wine. He'd been a tuba player in the Army, and he sang crazy old blues songs that made me happy.

He had left a wife and two little kids somewhere in Seattle before I'd even met him, and he didn't want to talk about them. I didn't either. I didn't want kids or want to care about anyone else's kids. I'd had enough of that with my little siblings, and that day on his borrowed motorcycle, flying up hills and across the bay, he'd won my heart.

He had done the harvest before and knew all about getting on as a driver; he would drive a pea truck, and I would sit at a conveyor belt, checking for sticks or mouse parts as the peas cascaded toward the machines which packed them into little boxes for freezing. I felt excited about going back to Oregon, where we would work the summer season and save enough for a car. It would be my first real job, and now I needed money. That was new, too. I'd never needed money before; it always came so easily to me as allowance for working for my mother during my teen years at home after Daddy's business finally took off. I couldn't quite imagine a factory with me in it, working for paychecks. I was curious and eager.

"We'll be coming to the border pretty soon," the man said, "and you guys 'll be fine. I'll say you're coming to Montreal with me, and from there you're taking a bus." It was dark by the time we pulled into the border station, and the Mounties weren't concerned at all about us sitting in the pickup. I worried that we'd be denied entry with only sixty-some dollars, no real destination, no real way to get across the continent, but the border guy only shined a flashlight into the cab and asked how long we'd be staying. Steve's smile, my smile, and "Just traveling through," seemed to satisfy them.

His warm body by my side, arm up over my shoulders, made me feel safe. I'd go anywhere with him just for the fun of it. What the hell else was there to do? No way to go but forward.

By morning, two more rides had gotten us to the middle of nowhere again. This time no mosquitoes, but the broiling sun and the dust started getting old after a couple of hours. Alternating pacing with standing and sitting on the rolled-up sleeping bag, I was seriously thirsty, tired, and angry at all the cars that zoomed on by. Things got so quiet I could picture a map of Canada with me and Steve as a pinpoint, traveling at a snail's pace. The dust was drying my feet to leather, and I was picking away at a sliver of glass in my heel when a car with two young guys zoomed by, one leering and hanging out the window laughing.

God, it made me mad to see them leave us in the cloud of dust they'd stirred up on the road. "Fuck you, you assholes," I screamed, trying out the new language I was rapidly picking up from Steve; running out into the road, I flipped them off in their old Chevy, which was about the umpteenth car to cruise by as if we didn't even exist. "What the hell are we gonna do if no one stops?" I demanded. Steve was tossing pebbles overhand into the woods as if it entertained him, long shots like from the pitcher to center field, and graceful. Just looking at the way he threw stones calmed me, but I also felt creeping, hungry-angry doubts about the wisdom of our plan.

"They will, don't worry. Someone always does." He acted as if waiting were just part of the deal, standing around patiently, throwing rocks and pebbles, stretching, yawning. He'd hitched before. He was a Leo and he waited like a lion, royally bored, certain of his inherent superiority—despite having only had one short ride since morning to this middle-of-nowhere country road.

"Uh-oh," I said, as the Chevy stopped, slammed into reverse, and roared backwards in curves to where we stood watching. The two guys were looking out the open window at us now, and I thought maybe we were in for big trouble; the one riding shotgun grinned and opened the door, scooting forward to pull the seat towards him, an invitation for us to climb in. I had some misgivings, but anything was better than one more minute in that same spot of hot, dry highway.

"Where y'all going?" the driver asked, sounding Southern while he stuffed his mouth with sandwich. They were kids my age, just out of high school, I guessed.

"West," Steve answered, "as far as you can take us would be great, man. Hey, thanks for stopping."

The shotgun guy looked back at me with a big smile. "Well, when we hear a little lady talking like that, we figure she must really need a ride." He grinned at the driver as if hearing a girl say "fuck" was really very entertaining. He stressed the "really" and kept grinning at me. Jesus, I thought, don't Southern girls ever swear? I knew I'd learned the word from Steve, though. No one I knew talked like that back home. North Eugene High School was clean and white-bread.

I was truly grateful that someone in the entire morning had manners, however, and I smiled, feeling embarrassed at my own swearing, which I wasn't really so used to, either. I averted my eyes to look out the window. "Thanks. We've been here for hours and no one would stop."

The driver waved his sandwich in his right hand and nodded to Steve, "There's fixings in that bag by the little lady's feet, and you all just make yourself some sandwiches and grab a drink."

Nice people, I thought; thank God for nice people. "Hey, thanks a lot. Are you sure?" There were Cokes and bread and bologna and lettuce in the bag of groceries at my feet, and I put together two sandwiches and relaxed, letting the breeze blow my long brown hair around. The dry wind felt good, like childhood summers when my father would drive our family down the Redwood Highway through construction stops, dust covering everyone and everything in the heat.

It wasn't so hot once we were moving, and it was a quiet ride for an hour or so. The guys didn't want to talk; they just listened to the radio and talked to each other a bit. It turned out they were kids from the States, too, headed to an uncle's ranch way up north to look for jobs. They dropped us at their turn-off, and we only waited briefly this time.

The next ride was a man going home to his farm in northern Ontario, who invited us for the night. They were having a barbecue, the man said, and Steve and I would be most welcome; he'd bring us back to the main road at dawn. The guy seemed decent and sincere, and I was so tired it sounded perfect to go to a party and then have a place to sleep and bathe and eat. Why the heck not, if the man was so generous? And there were no real plans for eating and sleeping along the way; it was going to be whatever came our way, whoever's path we crossed.

These people lived in a paradise house with bright green grass sloping down to a small lake; aspens and willows drooped into the water around the shore. The man who'd picked us up was a dad about my own dad's age, and he took me and some of his guests out in his canoe to fish and paddle around before dinner, something I'd never done with my own dad. This family seemed happy to be together. I loved the part near the shore, floating quietly under branches just coming into full leaf, filled with sunset light. I was too shy to say much to anyone else in the canoe, and very tired, but the evening felt lovely, like being in a painting. The kind man let me sit and enjoy the scenery, no questions asked.

At dinner his wife, who had soft, dark hair arranged in a twist at the neck, gave Steve and me a very close look. We were sitting in a formal dining room, formal but cozy too. A mahogany china cabinet was stuffed with collectibles—something my wannabe-fashionable mother would've turned her nose up at—and gleaming dark-wood chairs sat randomly against walls. The woman was on my left at the corner of the table. By her slight smile, I knew she was registering the difference in Steve's and my ages.

She asked me, "How old are you?" and I lied, adding two years, afraid that seventeen was just as illegal there in Canada as in the States. I had graduated high school at sixteen but couldn't explain all that. It would be better, I decided, to act old enough, like I had confidence in myself. The woman was looking down at her food and seemed kind like the husband, eating with us in her dining room. The others had eaten already. She was younger, I thought, than my own mom, or maybe just more relaxed, prettier and more at ease with her womanliness. "Don't you think you should head home after this adventure?" she persisted, taking a motherly stab at rescuing this teenage, vagabonding girl from the fully adult male. I heard in her voice a warning that things, maybe Steve, looked like trouble to her, but I knew I wouldn't bail out of the silent pact we had, at least not yet. The plates of potatoes and green salad, rolls, juicy meat, and fruit salad became the focus of my attention. I felt glad that listening to a lecture would be optional. If we had to we could just walk away, but I bowed my head toward the food and hoped the woman would let the subject go. I felt fairly happy with Steve, and the eight years he had on me were part of that comfort level. He'd been around, and I wanted to learn from him—how he managed. He loved life in his own silly way, everything from weather to pebbles to random art and music and me, and that's what I wanted. We were renegades already, almost two months together on the road. I looked at him sitting beside me, enthusiastically devouring the home-cooked meal. My own mother wouldn't want me back anyway, I thought; she didn't really care where I was, as far as I could tell, nor did my father.

"No, I won't go back," I told the woman, looking up into her dark eyes, briefly acknowledging the warning. "We're going to work in the pea harvest, in Oregon." I looked at her again, proud that we had a goal, proud that I'd stick to my plan of not having a real plan, of not going home again to parents lost in the oblivion of their cocktail hour.

My mother was annoyed and upset that I'd run off with Steve, but she hadn't tried very hard to stop me. I felt a wave of longing for someone besides this Canadian woman to care where I was or what I was doing—my stomach felt an alien seed of fear which I didn't want to acknowledge; there wouldn't be room for fear in my adventures with Steve. I devoured the rest of the dinner and thought about going home to tell my mother I loved her anyway, somehow, some way. But there was no way—there was no connection. I was an encumbrance to her. She needed my bedroom for my little sis. She needed to have fewer kids in the house, apparently. We could at least have a drink together one day, a meal and maybe some cocktails on the patio.

The woman gave me another deep look which I felt seep in, the kind my mother had never indulged. Now, if you were my mother, I thought but didn't say, I might have something to go back to. After dinner, the woman generously gave us an extra sleeping bag, to keep, and showed us to a little room with a soft carpet, a den I supposed, from the books and the chairs.

We were just about asleep when a knock came on the door; one of the guests from the barbecue entered and squatted down beside Steve's bag. We both sat up, fully clothed, to hear what he was telling us about, a train that came through at midnight. The guy, backlit in the light from the hall, looked like an English teacher I'd had in ninth grade—dark, short hair with a beard. He said, "You know, if you want to get across Canada fast"—he was pointing his finger now, as if we'd known there was a train that would stop just blocks away—"be over there at midnight when the Royal Canadian comes through." I was thrilled by the idea of a train ride at midnight, and one with a royal name, although it seemed scary, too. The man went on to tell us about getting on the second engine. "The train stops for water for about ten minutes, but it'll have a couple of extra engines back-to-back that ride along behind, and no one's ever in the last one."

"Well, how do you get in an engine?" Steve asked, sounding interested in the possibility; we'd already spent two days just getting to Ontario and were way farther north than we should have been—and we had no map of Canada. I felt assured by his asking for help.

"Get on the south side; it'll come on the third track," the man said, "and when the train stops—you'll hear the long whistle blow just before it stops—there'll be a ladder up the side of the engine and a little door that should open. Get in and get on the floor and stay down until you're outta town." We looked at each other in the light streaming in from the hall.

"Well, thanks for the tip. We'll talk about it," Steve told the man, who went out and closed the door. We decided to wait a bit, then pack up and slip out the window.

At the watering stop, just a few blocks in the direction the man had pointed, we huddled together out of sight in the grass by an outbuilding, watching, waiting in the cool spring breeze, and sure enough, the whistle blast and the noise of the train were right on time on the third track; it stopped with a great screech of brakes. Steve darted out first, and I followed in the moonlight to the ladder, which was silver like the engines which, just as the man had said, were the last two cars of the train, and gleaming.

Not bad, our own car, even if it is backwards, I thought, glad that Steve was sure they didn't shoot you for trespassing on trains. Jail maybe, but no bullets, he assured me. I looked around and saw not a soul; the small buildings were all on the other side. Steve went up first and slipped in the little door with the pack and one bag. I tossed the other bag to him and scrambled up the rungs. The engine's interior was cab-like, something like a car or boat. Two padded seats sat high off the floor so each rider could have a full view through the wrap-around front windows, which, of course, were pointing toward the track behind the train. There was a tiny door under the panel of dials and controls that led to the nose of the engine and another tall door that opened behind the two seats into the engine room itself. As we looked around from our positions on the floor, both leaning against opposite sides of the car, we laughed with relief. One thousand miles, the man had said. One thousand miles to Calgary, where we'd get off and hitch down to Idaho and over to Oregon.

We laid one sleeping bag behind the two seats, on the floor next to the door that led into the back of the car, and slept very close with the other bag opened over us. The engine, which was now a caboose, rocked and rolled along the rails. With my ear to the floor, I would have found the thundering noise of the wheels uncomfortable if I hadn't been so dead tired.

We awoke the next morning to sunshine and what seemed like quiet, no sounds but the engines and the rails. When I peered out the window, I realized we'd been riding already about eight hours, hadn't gotten caught, and were seeing something special: a zillion miles of virgin forest broken only by the train, as if we had been dropped back in time, just evergreens and a winding track behind us. From some of the curves we could see out over treetops, and the forests looked like rolling oceans going on forever and ever. I also realized we hadn't thought of food or water. "We're gonna get hungry," I said to Steve questioningly. He said we would find something, somewhere.

We established a bathroom area in the nose of the engine, where we were fortunate enough to find a gallon-size can that some conductor must have used for a spittoon. It was hideously noisy down there and dirty, but it would work for a hiding place, too. There were open spaces on the sides of the nose where we could see the ground speeding along under us. I found that when the train snaked around a curve, we could be seen if we were at the window, so we were careful about what we dumped and when. I decided that peeing out the engineer's window would be superior to trying to use the can, but we could only go for it when that side of the window was on a wide, outside curve.

We'd been awake for hours: standing up, sitting down, and moving into the nose at the watering stations when we could feel the train slowing down. After sharing our only food, an orange that I'd bought on Canal Street, the thought of two days on the train loomed like a long, long, time. We didn't have a plan yet for how to get water or a meal, but that didn't seem as important to me as the fact that Steve hadn't really held me or touched me since we'd left New York City. I was leaning against the tall, skinny door in the back of the cab, wrapping my arms around myself. "Hey," I said, but he only glanced at me for a second. It didn't seem right that he was acting so distant and moody all of a sudden, and here we were alone together with not much else to do, nothing that I could figure except watch a zillion more trees. He was sitting looking out the window as if I didn't exist, and it was really starting to bug me that he wouldn't notice me. For the first time since I'd known him, there was an uncomfortable silence between us. From the vantage point of now, I can sympathize that maybe the thought of sex with jailbait in public places might have quenched his normal ardor, but back then I had no respect for squeamishness.

I moved over to the engineer's seat he was slouched in and ran my fingers up his biceps, the skin so much like my own in its soft texture but tantalizingly male, tantalizingly not my own, and attached to so much power. I wanted to be ignited by the power under his skin. "No, not now," he answered my unspoken request, surprising me totally, as if he didn't even feel my fingers on his arm. I'd never asked anyone for sex and hadn't expected a rejection. He seemed to be sulking as he looked out the window of the train that was hurtling us backwards across Canada, his booted foot up on the open sill, his wide square jaw nestled into his hand.

"Why not?" I asked, guessing that he wouldn't really be able to resist; after all, he'd pursued me through three states, risked jail for me already, abandoned life as he knew it—whatever that was—all for me. I knew, facing twenty or thirty more hours stowed away together in an extra engine of the Royal Canadian, that sex was bound to happen, and why not now in broad daylight, when it seemed like a good idea to me? We'd been making love without giving it a thought, at least I hadn't. He was so passionate, so natural, so easy.

"It's just not a good time," he said again, holding his face away from my gaze, his chin still propped in his hand, looking at the forest as if it interested him more than my body did. I wasn't about to accept a silly no—what kind of precedent would that be? I bent across his torso and kissed him on his reluctant but beautiful lips, and that was all it took, really.

We were on the sleeping bags behind the seats when the tall, skinny door we hadn't dared to mess with, the one that led back through the engine and on to the next car, and then the next, opened a crack; I felt the pressure as it pushed on my hip while we were in the thick of it. I was naked on my back with Steve on top of me, and as our visitor pushed on the tall back door of the cab, Steve collapsed in a frozen attitude, not looking up to see the audience. But I did. We were all frozen in time, just my eyes making contact with the conductor's.

The man was gray-haired and sturdy looking, and kindly, I hoped. His eyes locked to mine, expressionless. As soon as he couldn't easily open the door into the extra engine, he must have suspected stowaways. After all, it had been a Canadian gentleman who had told us how and when to catch the train. Half drunken with the effect of lovemaking, I was still aware that my eyes should hold out a prayer of innocence and mercy to this man.

All the man could see of us was the back of Steve's head, his face now tucked down over my breasts, his thick, wavy hair like Godiva's giving me some coverage. His arms had slipped under my back and head, and my arms loosely held him. The man seemed to decide on how to handle his discovery as I noticed his cap, the traditional overalls, a denim jacket. He surprised me by politely and without a word averting his eyes and solemnly backing away, closing the door as if he'd simply entered the wrong room. We jumped up in a panic, scrambling into our clothes.

"God fucking damn it!" Steve swore. "God damn it, damn it, damn it. That's exactly what I thought would happen." He was jumping up and down in a Rumplestiltskin kind of fit, tucking in his blue work shirt and looking down the way I loved to see him do as he buttoned up his bluejeans. But I didn't feel guilty; no way in creation had our disrobing and lying down together caused the train personnel to become aware of our presence. I wasn't that superstitious. Besides, shouldn't love and its expression have the highest value—shouldn't my own lover be willing to risk all for my love and affection?

"Well, damn it, too," I said. "It was pretty funny that he opened the door just then." I could see that Steve didn't think it was funny at all. "We've been on the train for hours without seeing anyone," I went on, "and then, bam, just like that," I snapped my fingers and laughed at the irony that sex would produce such a reaction. Steve wouldn't even look at me but was back to sulking in the engineer's seat. Now we were caught but the train kept right on rolling. I half expected a jolt on the brakes and a bunch of angry men storming through the narrow silver door, telling us to get the hell off their train, out in the middle of the endless forest we'd been winding through all morning. But nothing happened; it was just the two of us waiting and waiting in what I thought was fairly blissful cruising.

Hours passed before the little door opened again. Neither of us had a watch, but it was getting close to twenty-four hours since we'd eaten dinner or had water. This time we were both seated in the swiveling engineer's seats with our eyes riveted to the door as it opened. "Okay you guys," the man said, a different man. Neither of us breathed a word; we just looked at this person who might be both judge and jury. I figured the first guy must have been nice, too embarrassed to talk to us after seeing me naked like that and in the act. His buddy had been sent. "The train will stop at nine tonight for about twenty minutes, just enough time to run like crazy to a market that's open late. You'll be able to get some supplies." We were speechless, just nodding our heads in gratitude. "There'll be a depot and a street just north of it. Go left about three blocks down that street, take another right one block, and hurry." He tapped his watch. "Nine o'clock, twenty minutes." Without another word he turned to leave, then added, "And stay down when we're in the stations during the day."

"Thanks," I whispered as the door closed.

When the train came into the depot and stopped, it was dark. We knew it was the stop the conductor guy had told us about. I didn't want to run carrying our things all the way to the store and back; I was too afraid we'd miss it if I had to stop and catch my breath, so I waited, just down the ladder in the dark. There was no one on the platform, and even though Steve had told me to stay on the train, I waited with the pack and the sleeping bags at my feet, peering around, praying he'd get back before the big engines started moving again. As the "all clear" whistle blew, Steve came sprinting down the platform and followed me up the ladder with not a second to spare. We sat on the floor and divvied up the goods. Our feast was beyond delicious: canned pork and beans, two quarts of orange juice, and bread and bologna. There was milk for breakfast and apples, oranges, and peanut butter. We guessed we'd be on the train for almost another day.

When we climbed down in Calgary, it was noonish, bright daylight, and the paying customers were visible along the track, on the station side. There was no other way out so we jumped quickly, and I acted as if it were totally not us who had just done so. The station was true Old West style, but I tucked my head down and we walked quickly along. Only the one or two who had actually witnessed our scuffle down the ladder with our pack and bags could verify that we'd been stowaways on the backwards second engine trailing the Royal Canadian, a thousand miles across virgin forest, and they had turned their heads politely. As soon as our feet were on the ground, we were simply bums in the train yard. Once I was off the platform steps and meandering down the street, the fear of harassment and arrest lifted off my shoulders and I felt euphoric—we'd done it—we were a thousand miles closer to our goal and with a few bucks for a cheap hotel.

The streets were dusty; the architecture looked mostly wooden, two-story Victorians in the train station neighborhood. We found a hotel in the second block, and I waited on the curb while Steve went inside to see if we'd be welcomed. Mr. and "Mrs." were given a second-story room, one with lace curtains in the tall sash windows overlooking the street. An even quicker wedding of our names than I had thought. I sat alone outside, noticing even then a sad consequence of the tag-along woman. I seemed to be keeping a tally book of major deficits to the counter-culture I had willingly entered. It wasn't called that yet, of course, but I knew my path was way off the norm, and I also knew I hadn't a lick of choice in the matter—not at this point. The reward was a bathroom with a shower, old but fully functional, and a sloping double bed with an iron frame—all original vintage and fine with me. Shower and sleep we did. The rest of the weary, but it didn't feel wicked, just alive and living.

In the morning after a breakfast from a grocery bag, we walked to Main Street, found the highway out of town in bright summer sun, and headed south into the States. Canadians must have thought it the right direction for funky-looking kids, and we were over the border and headed due west to Walla Walla in record time.

Merimée Moffitt

The Pea Harvest

It was almost dark when the last car dropped us in the center of Weston, Oregon, our final destination: population 165; altitude flat; attitude, pea harvest factory town. The only intersection with a stop sign hosted a tavern on one corner, a café across the street, a store, and some general shops—a one-block downtown. But the tavern was hopping, and Steve went in to ask about rooms for rent, alone again; I was still seventeen and too young for bars. Luckily, the upstairs apartment over the tavern had just been vacated and, since it cost only one dollar a night, Steve paid up for a week and we had shelter.

It wasn't pretty, but I didn't care about pretty. Pretty had only gotten me nowhere, and nowhere was what I had to learn about, being all new territory—not school, not home, not like my mom's—not anything I'd ever imagined. Steve had said there'd be jobs for us in this nowhere, and I trusted fully that there'd be a job. At least for him, and maybe for me. Until we rented the rooms above the bar, it hadn't occurred to me that we'd also have to find a place to sleep, cook, and fuck, too—all the necessities of life besides the job. It struck me as damned fortunate that a room—just poof!—had appeared, and that we were allowed to rent it.

The living room had a patterned, rolling linoleum that I found it best not to look at too closely, having no desire to change its slightly gritty surface; and a sofa, scratchy, old, small, and gray. There were two windows with curtains of thin fabric that let in light from the neon tavern sign and in the morning, the light of the desert and the new day. The small kitchen with one window had a table with two chairs, a stove with four burners, a fridge, a sink, and an overhead bulb. The bathroom was just a toilet and a funky tin shower—but it all worked. Hurrah! The bedroom was off the kitchen with one dresser and a bed so bowled out we dismantled it and put the mattress on the floor. It was a corner room with two windows overlooking the desolate yard and alley behind; the lot next door had a tiny Airstream trailer sitting dead center, where, eventually, a cowboy would play his fiddle on the steps. This place would be home for a while, and I would be mistress of the house.

The first morning we were at the factory by dawn, signing clipboards—the list that Steve had emphasized as essential. There it was: my new name at the bottom of the "people wanting jobs," and I could check back daily. The trucks were already rolling 24/7, the machines of the factory grinding and slamming; the sign-up man said we'd probably arrived in time to work. They were still hiring, but it would be night shift. Both shifts were twelve hours: seven to seven, whether a.m. or p.m.

By the first check-back, after caramel sundaes at the café and yucky beans in the apartment, we landed a pair of 7 to 7's—pm to am—my first real job, and I was so happy. They didn't care about Steve's shoulder-length blonde mane: he was a farm boy and tall and built and he'd driven for them before.

On day one the supervisor showed me around a bit. Women on stools at the conveyor belts sat high in a loft a full story of metal stairs above the factory floor, checking for foreign particles as peas poured in streams to the vats that would send them to packaging. The boss started me at the end of the system: loading boxes, full ones, onto the last belt that would take them to the loading docks, boxes of cans of peas—sealed, labeled, heavy, and ideally without too many mouse limbs or twigs cooked in. I did that for a while, until some woman in a flannel shirt and jeans decided to put me in the freezer moving things around. Then came break time, for which I had no snack or money, just a jar of the horrid beans from the night before. I sat alone in the locker room, too embarrassed by my own foreignness and the jar of beans to sit at a table. One woman invited me to come out of the dressing room, but I just smiled and thanked her.

After break, I guess since I hadn't cried or died after a few hours in the freezer, I was told to go upstairs, introduced to the ladies at the belt, given a stool too high to fall off of comfortably, and told to put anything that wasn't a green pea into the bucket that hung on the edge. The conveyer belts were on an open grate floor, the stairs metal and steep, and the noise was daunting. Above us the trucks roared up to the wall on the higher ground behind the behemoth factory. The drivers (all male in 1964) dumped their loads of pods and vines into the churn that led to chutes that sent them plummeting down to us. We women dangled our fingers all night long in the two-foot-wide, three-inch-deep river of peas. I guessed some little lady would get a surprise when she opened the can for her hubby's meatloaf dinner, but we were to do our best to prevent that intrusion into those sweet and clean kitchens of our staid and stable society.

The woman across from me, and the one to my right, all of them, wore bandanas that tied up their hair like Rosie the Riveter's. These women may well have been Rosie's age, or Rosie's mother for that matter. They were local women, all way older than I was. "Where you from?" the one across from me asked.

"Eugene," I answered. "Portland." Even I didn't know where I was from, but I knew, and they knew, it was far enough—different from their pickup ride to the farm, a walk down the road, their dusty existence. The roaring of the belts, the screaming of machinery from every direction kept the conversations to a minimum. I had no idea what to say anyway, so I watched my fingers—wet with the juice of the cool green spheres that seemed remarkably clean. Whatever machine shook them out of their pods and sent them to us did a good job. I only got one little mouse arm in my entire six weeks of nights at the factory. And I never fell off the stool. And no one ever said a word to me. I sat alone at lunch with my weird food and cigarettes. My long loose hair was never forced into a Rosie-scarf. Loose hair, loose woman, or girl really—I would turn eighteen at the end of our first week of work. Just climb those stairs, dangle the fingers, watch the peas, two breaks, one lunch. Smoke on break. Don't fall asleep on the stool. Payday on Friday.

It didn't strike me as odd that Steve would want to buy drugs. He'd gotten us the weird freaky speed in Berkeley before we'd left California to go to New York, after all, a very wired, weird trip, and I should have learned my lesson then. Some guy came by our tavern apartment on a Saturday night we had off, the Fourth of July, maybe, with speed—Jimmy Larson from Seattle, also driving truck, who knew Steve from way back. Steve always knew people, and in Weston, Steve knew Jimmy Larson, kid drug dealer. Why would I question the wisdom of the person I'd chosen as my leader? My handler? My daddy? I didn't. Steve was by default and natural selection my compass across the seas of days and days and years to come of living one hour at a time without one for-sure clue of how or what to do. I'd failed at school—an honor student without vision or stamina. (Too busy starving for several years of thinness?) There had been no alternatives popping up and grabbing me. So I followed Steve like I'd followed my parents, blindly and faithfully, until they totally surprised me with abject, sudden, and total rejection. But Steve was the man with the plan. To him it was obvious. You work, earn money, and spend it on what you need and want. Simple. I couldn't think that way. Paths unfolded in my head like twisted pea vines, like the several ways to hitch out of Weston, Oregon. Like the venues I might have selected for life besides following a Nordic-looking he-man running back and forth across the country and down its alleys and endless dead ends. I was frozen with indecision and lack of belief that I was worth any effort at all, even my own, but we did have fun being daredevils, loving the best we could. I was glad, furthermore, that I wasn't alone in a cold classroom, getting dizzy from the nothingness in my Portland fog, the Portland rain, a dorm room without comfort. At least he was warm and funny and handsome and welcoming of my close company.

But Jimmy Larson's speed was a real bummer of a plan. Maybe it was the man-sized dose, again, that they'd decided on for me—IV of course, no sissy stuff for these weirdos. Our little kitchen table and the two chairs became a sticky nucleus! After getting injected that evening (the act was repulsive to me and I wouldn't even look), Steve and I sat facing each other all night long—me paralyzed by the drug into one physical position while the fast train of methamphetamine ran wild circuits through my veins, and I thought the thoughts of someone else, someone who didn't need sleep or movement, except the movement of my arm bending to bring cigarette to mouth and hand to ash tray. All night long we sped through orgasmic conversations about nothing at all—humming together as if we were actually feeling the pace of the planet in our molecules. The rush of living fifty times faster than normal—just think! I aged two or three months in one night—the rush slowed down about dawn and then crashed to nil. Nothing and its other noun form: nothingness. Oh Jesus. By dawn I was psychotic.

When nothingness shifted to extreme paranoid delusions in the afternoon, Steve had already gone back to the factory for an extra Sunday day shift—no wonder he took the shit—he'd be working two twelves back-to-back, and as soon as Steve left, Jimmy's boyfriend showed up.

I stayed in the bedroom on the floor with my back to the door, worried that just because I'd witnessed Jimmy and his friend screwing on the sad little sofa, they'd kill me while Steve was out. I was so surprised to see two men fucking. Witnessing the act of homosexuality didn't bother me, but I worried and over-worried and got paranoid that they didn't want me to know. I hadn't been sure before that such an act existed outside of Italian novels. It wasn't my fault that I'd peeked out of my room and there they were, stacked up like plates face down on the sofa, looking at me silently as my door opened. At first, I didn't even get it. However, my eyes had to believe and had to get it. Would they kill me? Was someone going to kill me that very morning? Not only for using drugs, but also for seeing sex in this oddball form? My years of being tossed to the nuns, all those promises of hell for even thinking about sexual pleasure—that and my naïve nature was working overtime, short-circuiting synapses fried already with sleeplessness and foreign fluids in my veins. Did the rest of the town know what was going on in our little one-dollar-a-night pad? My mind created shadows across the windows and the plain white wall. I inched into the corner, too wired to sleep, too unnerved by the long night of rushing. Freaked to the max, I didn't like at all what the drug had done. Mental note: Do not shoot up speed with anyone, ever, anywhere again, no matter what anyone says. Note filed.

At dawn, Steve finally popped his head in the door and convinced me to get on the mattress with him, to chase the demons away with the comfort of his smooth and perfect, worry-free body. I had been in the corner scared and shaking for twenty-four hours.

The days and nights repeated themselves without drugs in Weston for the remainder of the six weeks, and Larson and his boy stayed away. Steve worked six nights, I worked five—all they would give me—but that was enough. The days were hot and on Sunday we'd swim at the river, lounge about the apartment, have caramel sundaes at the coffee shop on Main Street.

Uncannily, on the first morning after our very last night of work, after we'd been sleeping since returning home by 7:10 a.m. or so—the factory was three blocks down the street—I awoke to the noise of someone entering the living room and stopping at our open bedroom door. We were sprawled naked across the white-sheeted mattress in the bright, curtain-less room; crumpled top sheet and blanket on the floor nearby. By noon the bedroom always collected enough sun for us to sleep as if we were sunbathing on our own private beach.

"Daddy?" I could barely believe my eyes. My father had entered our universe, at least four hundred miles away from his and Mother's family home in Eugene, where no one slept nude that I knew of, and no one worked all night.

"Hi," he said. "I'll just wait out here while you get dressed." I was speechless. Too bad about being naked; our combined long-haired heads hadn't exactly concealed us in modesty, and he'd really gotten an eyeful, but hey, there is such a thing as knocking on a door. Jesus!

"Nice apartment," he said as his second greeting, in the snide voice he usually reserved for my mother. I ignored it as unintentional—too stupid to even respond to—as if moving to Weston had been an attempt at stylish living. He didn't get it.

"Yeah, well, what're you doing here?" I retorted back. My dad had disappointed me a few times, but not often enough for me not to be able to speak with him. I had the general opinion that he was funny at times, and very smart—at least bookish-smart. And he made funny faces at the dinner table after we ate, just often enough for me to know he could break the ice that crusted up between generations, and maybe between him and Mother, if he wanted to, but they basically didn't like each other much, as far as I could tell. He'd take his glasses off and rubber his lips around with his eyes all screwed up in his head—it was hilarious from someone so huge and potentially pompous. But this morning he was in the pompous mode—guess they weren't having much fun at the old homestead on the golf course without me around.

"Well, your Mother and I," he started.

Okay, I think to myself, that means Mother telling him what to think about me because no good news ever came from him with this preface of "Your Mother and I," like when "they" thought I should break up with my first boyfriend as we were getting "too serious." My mother always thought I was a slut even when I wasn't.

"Your Mother and I," he went on, "think maybe you're having mental problems." He was seated on the funky sofa, legs crossed, foot swinging, as if he were perfectly relaxed and enjoying his visit. I was in a kitchen chair across the room trying to listen carefully, having no initial idea of what would bring him so far so unexpectedly. Steve started making coffee and stayed in the kitchen.

"I want you to do me a favor," he went on. "We want you to come to Portland to see a psychiatrist we've contacted, just see him for a consultation, and then I'll drive you back here." My mind clicked immediately to "free ride to Portland" with all our collected junk, which had grown to more than a backpack-full.

There was no feeling of remoteness between me and my father, in spite of the situation. Daddy had always been part of our regular routine: he had his chair to read in after dinner, and sometimes we'd bring him cookies and milk—at least a goodnight peck on his whiskery cheek, and he'd look up, pleased. Our family home had a big beige leather chair and ottoman known as Daddy's chair, but it was open to us all if he wasn't home. There was a coffee table, an ashtray, and a nice reading lamp. He read political science books and history and had a wall of all kinds of books in the den, floor to ceiling. He'd graduated at the top of his class.

I walked into the kitchen to ask Steve. "Do you want to take the ride to Portland?" His opinion would be mine, yet my own feelings were clear. A ride was a ride, and we wouldn't have to hitch or spend money on a bus. We weren't likely to take a bus—much cheaper and more fun to hitch.

"Sounds okay with me," he said, doing something at the stove. He had a day's work still but he wouldn't mind missing it. Perhaps he was just being agreeable since he had indeed run off with me, and my father had driven so far to ask this favor.

There was an new awkwardness with my father—a new space created by my living with Steve, by my hitchhiking across Canada, by my working in a factory for six weeks, by the sight of the two of us naked and asleep in tan healthy bodies, sprawled innocently in the afternoon sun. Were we insane? Was I? I wasn't afraid of a psychiatrist, though I might have been if I'd known what my parents actually had in mind.

"Okay, we'll go with you, but you won't need to bring us back. We were going anyway in a couple of days." It seemed so odd to negotiate anything with my father, who'd never worked out plans with me before. He simply said it was okay if Steve went too, and that he'd pick us up at eight the next morning. "Bye," I kissed his cheek. "See you in the morning." It was the best I could do, and he drove off to whatever town he was staying in, Walla Walla probably.

I had no sense of wanting to be rescued—of needing rescue. Steve and I as a couple, we were the rescue. My parents were the swamp, the Slough of Despond I needed rescuing from, and Steve was my shining knight. It wasn't like I ever used the word love. We weren't in love; we just liked each other. I was comfortable with him, like graphite particles up against an anvil. His face and energy met mine and we melded, we moved, ate, slept, fucked, worked, shopped, breathed, did everything as a twosome. I didn't understand any of the previous labels I'd been taught, all of which had resulted in me being abandoned and homeless, essentially, in a country that mind-napped my male peers and sent them to be killed for no apparent reason. That much I knew. And that same country had no reasonable plans for women except as indentured servants who would take up booze to ease the humiliation of being second-class citizens in their so-called marriages.

Steve and I were a couple, as far as I knew—that was more or less an unspoken pact between us. Perhaps neither of us dared to define what we were doing, but I was without a leg if I was without him. Of course, that was probably the seed of the disintegration right there. He must've gotten darned sick of having to plan my life and see to it that I was moving and eating and breathing. But that came later.

Some ride. Lots and lots of silence, like the pea factory, and our trip across the continent was of no interest to my father at all. What was I to him? A danger to myself or society so much that I had to be locked up? "We think you may need to be put into a hospital," was all he said as he rolled on alongside the Columbia River, and I knew that wasn't going to happen. My brain was too clear and functional. I didn't for one minute think they'd find me lock-up-able. I wasn't worried. I promised Daddy I'd do the doctor thing and go along with it all. He said that they, too, would go with the doctor's recommendation.

It was embarrassing to see our things wrapped in the white sheet, tied up as if we were real hillbillies, Steve in the back with his arm along the top of the back seat, grinning like the world was his apple, his hair, my hair flapping in the warm wind as we zoomed down the Columbia Gorge on into Portland.

Merimée Moffitt

Goose Hollow

My father drove us right up to Nick and Maryalice's front door in Goose Hollow—it may as well have been Appalachia or Tahiti; as an old neighborhood in Portland, it had the exotic allure of a destination. The house had a deep, worn front porch and two or three stories of Victorian rooms all filled with the junk that Maryalice so diligently collected: turn-of-the-century desirables like raggedy old dolls in lace and satin dresses with beyond-stunned looks on their porcelain faces, umbrellas and stands, rugs, chairs, curtains, everything old, elegant, musty, lots of mahogany. Nick's contribution was music and the people who played the blues and sang with him—the bass players, other guitarists, singers, harp players, stand-up bass players—their faces appeared from day one.

Steve and I were given living-room sofa-bed privileges, along with an offer the first night to do partner-swapping, which Steve nixed without hesitation after reading my head shaking no. I didn't even know these people and the idea frightened me, though I had met Nick in the pickup truck in San Francisco one morning with Steve. Nick had won my heart with harp-playing and song, but Nick was greasy and slick, a white-blues-player unsavory look, button-up shirt and vest, John Lennon glasses. I wasn't at all ready to be bartering material. Maryalice had the skinny, flat-chested, beatnik beauty—bony face, blonde hair to her butt, the humorless gaze—all down pat. I was so relieved when Steve said no way man, forget it. I hadn't liked being discussed, being considered tradable, anyway. Nick's body was not a turn-on—I didn't know at the time that it was drugs, his addiction oozing out of him.

My dad picked me up the first morning and dropped me off for my agreed-upon psychiatric testing; I promised to call him and Mother to discuss the results. The old-dude shrink had gnarled, ancient hands and a face to match his antiquated notion that I was a specimen, one of these "lost girls" out misbehavin' in the world. My inkblot and Rorschach tests had read "loony," apparently—the report said borderline personality disorder and needing outpatient therapy three times a week.

"But I can't work with this guy, Mother. He creeps me out; he's an asshole," I told her on the phone. As usual, she wasn't up to a conversation. She habitually selected an annoyance like a hunter picking out a fat bird in a flock; I could almost hear the hammer clicking back as she set me in the crosshairs. I was swearing! Oh, my! I was asserting my new life, my new vocabulary. At least the shrink told my parents I wasn't so crazy that I had to be locked up. He said I would be ready, though, for intervention, for the bin—"Girl, Interrupted" in the making—if I were to go untreated.

My mother, angry instantly at my lack of acquiescence, said, "Well, I guess then that we have nothing to say to each other," and she slammed the phone down on me—I was at a pay phone and I had no more change. And she didn't call back. That was it! End of family. I had called the guy an "asshole," which must have translated to her, "I'm not going to be you, Mother. I won't just do what you or Daddy or some random guy tells me to do to keep me on the track that leads to a miserable life like yours."

And that was that—no treatment, no more parents. But it was only a mild shock. My parents had never had much success at communicating anything of interest to me. Age eighteen and six weeks, thank God for those six weeks; I don't think I understood that my mother was actually attempting to disown me and incarcerate me all in one fell swoop—as if she'd ever really owned me anyway. The funny part is that she didn't know what the heck she was doing either. A couple years later she missed me, wondered about me—as if there'd never been a disconnect on her part.

Poor mom, not having fun. Too much booze, I'd say—and Daddy, he liked to insult her for being a housewife—one who served him and worked for him round-the-clock. It seems that when Hitler came along, quite a few folks decided that getting hitched and having sex and babies was top priority. Does every generation of women fall for that? Is that why men create these wars—to scare women into hasty marriages? When she did get around to missing me, my friends found her ad in the Portland paper for me to call home, but it wasn't any different. Nothing had happened or changed. I called; nothing I said mattered. I was asked not to call again, not to drop by, not to come home for Christmas. That went on for four years. I have no recollection of what eventually made them change their mind and re-own me, maybe the family therapy they tried. Maybe my brother interceded, his opinion being that I was saner than either of them.

Steve rented us a gem of an old house—all gingerbread with a wraparound porch—on the edge of a small park east of Barbour Boulevard in Southwest Portland. Then he started driving cab for grocery money while I stayed home playing with oil paints, making self-portraits that quickly bored and depressed me. He built us a swinging bed, but I just felt like a monkey in a cage. The place had all the original gas fixtures, and Steve blew his eyebrows off going up in the attic to fix a leak to the wall sconces and gorgeous old chandelier. He used a match to find the leak in the gas pipe. Blew a hole right through the ceiling and came back down without any eyebrows. The ennui of being his had begun.

School had failed; I didn't understand working and independence, wasn't interested in cooking or anything, really. But before it dawned on me that that's what people did to get along, another drug trip came along which derailed our little home life near the park before it could even get going.

Nick came over and got in bed with me one day when Steve was at work, just climbed right in, and it wasn't pleasant. "Come on, baby—just let me get next to you. I want you so bad," or some such bull, and I was right about that greasy, unsavory thing. It was awful and he called me "talented" as if I were a whore. No whore just gives it away, but I was learning about "giving," I suppose. He seemed angry and resentful that I had "given" him what he claimed to have wanted just because he'd asked so many times I was tired of hearing about it. Then he came back a few nights later with cocaine for me and Steve that he and some junkies had stolen from a drugstore, pure pharmaceutical cocaine, and that was far more pleasant than the sex on his last visit. Was it pay for my services? Was it to shut me up? To make up, say he was sorry? To dig me in deeper into their hole with them? Cocaine gives an uncanny, unreal sense of pleasure within the skin—the way we'd like to feel, the way we imagine Adam and Eve may have felt before the Fall. Bliss just standing there, bliss leaning against a wall, bliss at having a body. We got so high, so ripped on that stuff, that by dawn we'd decided to pack all our things into our newly purchased black Chevy sedan and drive to California, to the wine country where it was sunny and warm. We were running from our coming-down, and/or the police, I eventually supposed. We had Nick in the car with us, too, since Maryalice had given him the boot for the umpteenth time, and it turned out he had a heroin habit he would have to kick also. By dawn we were in Sonoma County, stopping for doughnuts and gas.

Steve went to work at Louis Martini's wine-making barn in Saint Helena every morning while Nick and I hung out in the great skeleton of an empty, turn-of-the-century dream house we rented in Calistoga. With nothing to put in it, no sense of really living there, the house was spooky. Sometimes, if I wanted to spend a bit of Steve's dough in the grocery store, dinner and all, I'd drop him off and then come back at four like a good wifey-poo to pick him up. I was almost happy on some of those fall afternoons. The drive was gorgeous as wine country simply is, and the weather warm; Steve's boss would give me the appreciative eye, and even gave me a tour of the place as if I were a normal human. But there was nothing acceptable about what was going on in the old mansion.

Nick was going through his sweating and shaking stages, gray-looking and just plain sick every day. "God, what can I do for him?" I asked Steve, who'd been working for a week or two. He must have known something about withdrawals. Steve simply said to give him water. I'd go in Nick's upstairs room across the hall from ours with food or a drink, but I wasn't his designated nanny, and I wasn't about to get next to him much. Everything about that house was in shades of aging gray, peeling paint outside, powdery paint inside, bare floorboards, gray curtain-less windows, our dwindling sense of fun—and Nick's skin and hair and clothes and bed sheets matched it all. In our room, Steve and I had a mattress only, plain white sheets (going gray) and an open sleeping bag for a quilt (Army green). Our clothes overflowed in piles out of bags on the floor. Just traveling through—vagabonds.

There was a table in the kitchen and two or three pans, a few dishes—not much to make a home of. I read an Anna Karenina from cover to cover, lying on my belly in the light from the three tall windows, the trees in the yard even taller than the house; birches bordering the front yard on the main avenue that wound down from the hills. Steve's paycheck covered gas, rent, and food, but I didn't know what to do with myself. I didn't feel part of anything but this unsavory threesome. Didn't feel like I could go get a job and make a life out of hanging out in Calistoga. It seemed we were merely observers, still coming off that crazy cocaine trip I noted never to repeat. There was nothing I could imagine doing besides reading—the same way I'd learned to cope with my parents' frequent moves, bankruptcies, and continual uprooting. Life in suspension. No future, the past a burned bridge. Me as pretty wifey-poo with hair blowing in the breeze wasn't an everyday thing—in a bad mood after a full package of cookies for lunch, I looked like hell's fury anyway. Nonetheless, I still had no thoughts of my own on where to go, how to live, what to do.

Nick finally got out of bed after weeks of what may have been a near-death experience, and the seasonal nature of work at the winery made the decision for us. We left with a little dough and headed down into Berkeley to the Berkeley Hotel—a smart move on Steve's part, as there was no way I wanted Nick to lodge with us. Already back on the dope as soon as we hit civilization, he had to hit the streets and find his own way home elsewhere, without me or his good pal Steve.

The hotel looked out over a boulevard and our room had its own bathroom; we bought an electric frying pan to do our cooking in. Steve got the daily paper and showed me the want ads, hoping to help me find employment—what a good daddy he was. By the next week I was commuting to San Francisco to do file clerking in an insurance office. In a zombie-like trance, I'd eat a sack lunch on a bench in the financial district. Depression found me a warm and willing host.

    Steve took some time checking out the scene in Berkeley, locating other losers, bums, and drug connections while I did the lonely office-girl thing—solitary in the city, feeling more like a pigeon than an actual human living a human life—file clerking wasn't going to last long. I hadn't yet read Melville's Bartleby, but I certainly preferred doing nothing to slaving away putting papers into cabinet drawers all day. The claustrophobia of office air, the weird office girls with long nails and shoes that kept them focused on their feet, and depressed sex at night just didn't do it for me—I didn't get it. I suppose Steve had it coming; he deserved a few weeks of living on my checks after I'd simply read away the late summer and early fall while he hauled ass in the vineyards, but enough was enough. Nonetheless, my last paycheck secured us a bedroom in a little house on Woolsey Street with the nefarious Palmiter brothers, Larry and Alex. Our unspoken purpose would be to provide cover, to make the place presentable. Compared to Alex, who ran a meth lab in one of the bedrooms, and Larry, who dealt, or at least stashed kilos of weed in his bedroom closet, we were the essence of innocence, Adam and Eve in the garden. Were we? Was that what I was seeking, knowledge from the tree, the apple, and the snake's bitter bite? Or life as an irresponsible, wife-like Eve? Well, maybe.

Woolsey Street, Owsley, and LSD

I'd met Larry at Reed, where even I knew I'd gone to find beatniks. The school was snooty and expensive, but I had the grades and scores and my dad had said find a college. (His business of buying timber cheap and selling it dear was finally paying off.) The day I left for Reed, my father, showing off his new success in a very generous move, wrote me a check for tuition, books, dorm, and food, and handed me some spending money, which I was to bank and use as needed.

On our first date, Larry, the tall, lanky, already old-looking nerd/beatnik had spouted eternally boring facts about the plants and wildlife of what they now call the wetlands. Back then it was simply the canyon, acreage with a creek that fed an old outdoor swimming pool, charming under droopy willows, but there was no heat between me and Larry; I wanted eye-opening philosophies, hot sex, wild passion—something! But Larry was a file cabinet on feet. Failing to get any friction going between us, he had apparently sent word to

Seattle for Steve to come down to Reed and meet me, which I didn't find out about until decades later. Steve and I were fire and air, Leo and Gemini, and he was supposed to loosen me up, Cyrano me for Larry. God only knows what scheme these guys had in mind back in '64, and it's too late to ask them now.

Larry had been busy in the Bay Area since the Reed days, dealing weed from Mexico in an effort to turn on the world, Timothy Leary-style—"Turn on, tune in, drop out"—the beatnik credo first. His bedroom closet in the little bungalow on Woolsey Street was a mini-silo for the stacks of kilos. His roommate and brother, Alex, was the Berkeley meth king Steve and I had visited before our trip to New York in the drive-away car a year earlier. I had no idea Alex was manufacturing the stuff right in the house. He didn't leave the room, and I was never invited in. Maybe he just keeled over once a week. The one time I'd peeked in, there was a chem lab laid out on the hardwood floor but no bed; I didn't know what he did. I was eighteen and the definition of naïve. But the house never blew up, and the cops never came, lucky for us.

There were a few speed freaks Steve had to throw out the front door (crazy Brian Casey wrapped in a shower curtain—a shower curtain!)—the results of way too much meth. Steve had to boot the chair and Brian down the front steps. I suppose that was Steve's function and why we weren't even expected to pay rent; my function, of course, was cooking, cleaning, and being pretty (what a surprise). The two of us were healthy, sunny-looking types. The night Augustus Owsley Stanley III was to drop by for dinner, I just happened to be making my most dependable balanced meal: all-American meatloaf, salad, potatoes, and peas.

My first contact with Owsley was his hand on my ass as I was bending to the little shelf to get my salad bowl, but since it was Owsley's hand I decided to take it as a beneficent acknowledgement of my charms. I must've looked pretty hot in that red sweater dress, as even Rodney had said so that night, Rodney being an elegant, educated drug addict who usually maintained an aloof manner. Owsley asked for something to dump his powder into. "After dinner, you could use this," I said and held up my wooden bowl.

"Hey," he said, "do you wanna earn some money capping this stuff up?" He showed me a plastic bag full of white powder.

"Well, okay," I said. "Sure." We always needed money. Owsley wasn't a looker, but was interesting in his geeky-scientist way. He had on a tan trench coat, expensive-looking, and a nice white dress shirt. I'd heard he still worked at the labs. I liked being physically close to someone who had it together—a job, a career, money. It had been a while. I wanted him to fall in love with me and whisk me away from the misery of living with a madman and his crazy drug-fiend friends. The beggarly, starving lifestyle looked like a long road ahead for me, as I saw no way out. There was no niche in life I could imagine myself into, and there I was: as stuck as my mother in her country-club existence. I invited him to eat with us.

"Yeah, sure," he said. "That'd be great, and after I'll show you what to do."

The house was so adorably fifties—breakfast nook and patterned linoleum, dining room with mahogany table and chairs, living room with cozy sofa and easy chair and Larry's famous record collection and state-of-the-art, top-of-the-line sound system. Larry must've owned every Folkways record, every blues record, all the Motown and gospel singers, and all the rock produced through 1964. And besides getting high, the thing was to commandeer the sofa or the easy chair and really get into the sound system and record collection that Larry had put together. The living room was a social event where friends dropped by to get high and listen.

Owsley was a special guest, as even Alex came out of his meth-lab room. Usually one of his flunkies brought him food in a to-go bag. That night we devoured the meatloaf and all the fixings. I told Steve that we had a job capping the LSD powder, and he seemed pleased. It was Owsley's second big batch, but the first batch had paved the way. Some of Steve's friends had already heard of the new drug.

When the table was cleared and the salad bowl washed and carefully dried, Owsley ceremoniously dumped the pile from the plastic bag into the flat-bottomed bowl, a wooden bowl from Hawaii my mother had sent me. Steve and I sat attentively as Owsley explained how to scoop with one half of the gelatin cap, level it off, put a dab in the other half and snap them together. I wondered about milligram dosages as soon as we started and realized how utterly imprecise the filling of the gel caps would be.

It was a tedious job, and the ceramic bowl holding the finished caps was filling slowly. Owsley had gone home; Larry was around somewhere, possibly visiting Alex in the forbidden room. Larry, whose space was the back bedroom, was hiding from the feds on a drug charge related to "large marijuana distribution."

I wasn't thinking about much as I concentrated on filling the little caps as randomly as possible—some extra full, some with less, sort of like life itself, hoping the more stable types would buy the full caps. Steve sat in the straight-backed chair right next to me, and we just kept capping, dipping and capping. I'd had some of Owsley's very first acid in St. Helena that summer, and the drug had made me really fall to pieces—a major bum trip. It had been so weird, like my whole body was greasy and awful-feeling, as if I were garbage: sweaty and nervous and self-conscious. I'd been hyper-aware of how nowhere on the planet was really mine; a full-blown, instantaneous, and energized depression, as if I were some kind of extra in the planetary movie, without purpose or connection. Steve had gotten all over me, maybe thinking that would help. Hands, mouth, kisses, trying to snap me out of the grip of the drug, but it had been a daytime nightmare, not pleasant. Hardly sensual or psychedelic, just sad, which was often, back then, my default state of mind. The trip had left an indelible aversion to the new drug that Owsley wanted to pay us to push, so I wasn't planning on taking any. Looking back, it seems the St. Helena trip was a strong psychic slap to wake me up.

But Steve, a substance-using daredevil, loved drugs. He always tried anything available to get him off the personality and mindset that his farm-working Norwegian parents had raised him into. He'd told me about hating his family's rigid rules and punishments. His failed marriage and venture into parenting were never discussed. One thing the counterculture did that made sense to me was to not look back. Just to live on the edge like we did meant focusing on the now, maybe a few thoughts to the future, but we were dedicated to living in a minute-to-minute, day-to-day plan. Be Here Now, when it got picked up by the meditation crowds, would become a standard mantra for do-right hippies just a year or two down the road.

The dish of caps not even half done, Steve looked at me with an impish grin. His face was godlike as usual; I always liked the manly shape of his jaw and the chin with the little Nordic cleft, his sea-blue eyes. He inspired a trust by appearing to be so well-made, such a functional physical form. "Let's just taste a little of this—one little lick to see if it's the real thing," he said, his eyes looking into mine. I realized then, as he licked the tip of his finger then stuck it in the salad bowl again, that all of my fingertips were white, rubbed white evenly, and that the powder had probably entered my bloodstream already, right through the pores. I didn't need a lick. Waves of gospel music, the Swan Silvertones singing "Oh Mary Don't You Weep," swept over us from the living room. I looked at Steve as an almost-nausea hit my jaws and salivary glands. I had disliked how helpless the drug had made me feel before, and now I was feeling peculiarly not quite in my body again; I saw his eyes grow glassy and smiley and more and more remote. There was an "Oh no, I'm falling" feeling, which felt not so bad, as if maybe it wasn't going to be so horrible this time; then we simultaneously slithered from the straight-backed chairs, laughing, falling on each other like puppies in a heap and onto our backs on the hard carpet.

I promised myself to do better this time, not to get on the misery trip. We stretched out on the floor on our backs, as if we were astronauts getting ready for launching. I often thought Steve could think my thoughts and I his, and this was one of those times. Gospel music, acid in a bowl, drug dealers on the other side of the wall; it was too funny, and my eyes felt as if they weren't working right at all. We touched our heads together with our bodies making an angle, and I felt peaceful, just resting on the rug, staring at the ceiling, listening to the swooping, pulsing harmonies. I tugged myself up to look at his face, and he looked miles away, as if down the wrong end of a telescope, smiling at me, also peaceful, in his own universe near mine; I didn't think there would be any connection between us for a while because something was happening, an override to normal sensation. He couldn't help me, but I didn't feel scared, just alone.

Our bedroom was a glassed-in sun porch on the back of the bungalow, and I always liked the cool porchiness of it, the wraparound glass windows looking into an old garden. I started crawling in that direction, and he let me go, didn't say a word. I pulled myself to my feet at the doorway, not knowing why I was entering the bedroom, until my eyes fell on the scene out the window, and I walked slowly toward the wet glass. The wall of windows across the back of the dark bedroom looked into the wild, unkempt backyard with vines that had overtaken huge shrubs; the grass was deep and dewy. The yard glowed eerily in moonlight, and the window felt like the safest place to stand and simply feel myself stand—one thing at a time. Crawl, then stand. Thoughts flitted through me like birds hopping from branch to branch. No thoughts. Bird thoughts—flitting and empty, nothing bad or sad. I focused on the jungle of trees and bushes lining the yard's periphery that seemed to beckon in a way I hadn't noticed from plants before.

Each plant appeared to be vividly and intensely, individually alive and glittering, almost trembling with emotions and vibrations of its own, and aware of me. That was the odd part. They, the trees, were looking at me as I watched them. I was shocked at how active the backyard appeared to be. Rooted as they were, I realized that a clan, a tribe lived right there. I felt apologetic that I'd not recognized them before, humbled by my ignorance. Awed by the splendor of their being-ness. They shimmered as if wearing the Queen's jewels, and I felt an urge to go outside, even in the dark, cold, wintry evening, and simply be with them. They exuded a presence far more enticing than the houseful of men I lived with. I felt like one of them, too, a tree woman, standing in my bedroom window, not really wanting to move again, or do anything again, except maybe escape to the yard and be with these beings whose lives were so defined that they had no need for worry or fear. They seemed to be calling me.

"Are you okay?" I turned and saw tall, slightly stooped Larry silhouetted in the doorway. His back was to the light from the rest of the house, but he must have noticed me standing in the window, transfixed by the dark backyard, a silhouette also. His room was across from ours at the end of the hall. "Yeah," I heard myself say, softly. I felt the words coming up and out as if from inside an instrument, a violin or cello. "I'm fine." I liked how I sounded—a talking tree; a talking, human, tree. I had chosen to talk to Larry; the sense of choice gave me some feeling of strength, but I didn't want to break the spell.

"Well, come on back to the living room," he said, and put out a hand toward me. I felt like he was trying to lure me back from some precipice, or maybe he sensed my desire to flee. "We're going to smoke some really good weed," he said. I didn't like weed that much, but it was what they did, all of them, all the time.

He was standing there waiting for me, and I couldn't figure out an argument or how to say no. He was older than I was by about eight or nine years, as was Steve. I had gone off to college very young, barely seventeen, virginal, and Larry had picked me from the freshman class as if I were some kind of wild flower or comfy toadstool. He'd posed as an older student, and then later let me know that he hadn't actually been enrolled for years. He was a pedantic type who seemed old at twenty-five. But here he is now, I thought, maybe aware of my dilemma with the yard and the plants and the humans. I felt a wave of anguish because I could think of absolutely nothing else to do or say. Sitting with the trees in the cold, rainy night just wasn't going to fly with anyone's perception of how I should "be." At eighteen and for a long time to come, I still aimed to please.

"Okay." I crossed around the end of the double bed and stepped into the doorway with Larry, the old awareness of how I'd rejected his advances still lingering. My body felt light and comfortable. I appreciated the kindness he was showing by escorting me down the hall, away from a potential lonely freak-out. The drug was giving a pleasant effect. He let me walk in front of him as if to scoot me along, to keep me from forgetting where I was going.

Steve patted the scratchy fabric of the old rose-colored plush sofa, and I slipped into place next to him, knowing that my prettiness lit up the room, that my red dress was warm and sexy. The rest of the evening was laid out in a familiar pattern: smoke, listen, sit, bed, sex, sleep. Easy, but I felt good inside; I'd managed to get high on the new drug and not have an awful trip. Success in my peer group. The little exodus from normalcy had passed, even if the walls and the rug were slipping into waves and paisley patterns with the music. "Nice cleavage," Rodney said as he leaned down from the center of the room to pass me the joint, and that was my role, to sit and be pretty. I didn't have much to say.

When we went to bed, Steve felt warm and strong as usual. The dark room was close to the trees and they were a comfort. It wasn't bad, not bad at all. Sex and sleep.

Owsley came back the next morning to collect the caps and settle with us for our work, and we were almost finished when he showed up. Steve had gone out early and bought thin rubber gloves so we could finish the capping. Owsley gave us fifty caps and fifty dollars in pay and three hundred fifty caps to sell, wholesale. That would mean we owed him a thousand dollars, I realized with some apprehension. If we sold the hits for five or six each, we could earn enough to live on for a while and pay our expenses. The math made sense, and Steve agreed to take the caps out of the neighborhood, then to return to Berkeley to pay Owsley and possibly continue with another batch. A plan. Part of the deal was that we would head north and sell the acid in Portland and Seattle.

Larry and Alex decided about that time, also, that Woolsey Street was getting too hot and we all should disband. I sensed there was heat on Larry: I'd heard some mumbled private conversations about narcs sniffing around; someone had reported to the brothers about something. The morning Owsley gave us our pay in caps it was time for us to split entirely. I could feel the urgency of having so much still-not-illegal LSD and the stark danger of Larry's closet of weed. Someone might want any of it bad enough to come get it from us. Time for us to go, right away—no thinking or lollygagging about. Steve and I said our goodbyes before the brothers even started packing—I wasn't about to help, worried that any minute squad cars would swoop in and cart us all off to various jail cells—uh-uh. I wanted to get away from the place. There was a bit of well-wishing on the front steps, but I wanted out of there before a bust, not after. Our bags were packed, and the little black Chevy's trunk and back seat were full. We would drive to Portland, then Seattle, to ply our wares.

Merimée Moffitt

Leaving Steve the First Time

Things were deteriorating in every way back in Steve's hometown of Seattle, where we drove from freak's house to freak's house as if we were selling Bibles. Generally the male head of household or one person would be Steve's contact, but most were people Steve had met while at U of W. Maybe they smoked a little weed if they were musicians or writers; it was 1965 and hippies hadn't sprung up organically yet. This was a test batch meant to whet the appetites, to get the thing going, which eventually it did. Steve kept coming up with just enough dough to get us through the day, and then the next, then the next, and so on, so we certainly weren't saving the thousand bucks we owed Owsley for the bag of caps, giving away at least as much as we could sell. People had never tried it, and they wanted free samples. Always the free samples. Steve wasn't much of a salesman, and I, of course, a tag-along woman, just watched. Most people wanted to see if they liked it before they'd pay five bucks. So we Johnny LSD-seeded around the scene, donating to every old friend and everyone we thought might like to try the new "psychedelic" tripping drug. It was depressing to say the least: homeless, kitchen-less, not a bed to call our own. Steve couldn't get anyone to pay for something he just kept giving away. We were trying to live on the new fast food, nineteen-cent hamburgers and sacks of greasy fries. Steve finally parked me in a tiny house and drove back to the Bay Area, supposedly to get to Mexico to score some kilos—he gathered down payments for that—playing the high-roller drug dealer now, but when he returned, all he had was a little rosewood coffee table he thought I'd like.

Alone in the tiny house, I was crocheting hats for my family for Christmas and trying to live one day at a time, keeping warm by an old freestanding gas heater. There didn't seem to be a future—the rain was a constant, the cold, the nothingness of being a woman. All the guys had instruments, but we'd hawked my guitar and Steve had told me I couldn't sing worth a damn, anyway. I felt like a child in an empty day care whose mommy had forgotten to return. Sex and drugs and rock 'n' roll proved fairly boring as I was always just a concession-provider—oh yeah, they liked that I could cook, and liked that I looked pretty, and Steve liked getting close to me but we didn't talk enough, we had no plans, and the sex was like it was happening to someone else. I was barely in my body—it was not an okay life, and at this point I had been left alone for too long.

And so I bailed on him one day: took the old De Soto coupe we'd bought when the Chevy broke down, the cash, my suitcase, and headed for New York. Our mutual acquaintance, Mac, asked if he could come along; he had a wife in New York City and wanted to see if she'd take him back. Mac had been more or less living in Alex's meth scene and our paths had crossed just as I'd decided to get away from Steve. I'd been enchanted from day one with Mac's coffee-colored skin, pale green eyes, and long, lanky, athletic body. Incredibly good-looking, and incredibly addicted to meth. Totally bad news, but I was curious about all the "news" (things that were new to me), even what made this guy bad. How bad could bad be, especially if packaged in an angel's body? Never any worse than the straight scene my parents called life, booze and their crazy war. It wasn't that I left Steve because of Mac Macomber; it's just that he was there in Miki's kitchen, saw me heading out with a suitcase and a car and asked if I'd take him home to New York. Maybe he wanted to beat his habit while driving penniless across the USA with a bimbo like myself, and I had absolutely no measuring gauge with which to determine whether Mac was high-risk, low-risk, or mostly fun like Steve before the drug peddling job got too boring and pitiful for me to tolerate. I wanted out—Steve and I were at a dead end—he didn't seem to mind, but I did, and at least New York, again, was a destination. Maybe on my own, some magic would happen.

Halfway across New Mexico in the red-and-white two-door that Steve had found for fifty bucks—Mac and I were going Route 66 after stopping in Berkeley for his belongings—after hours of driving and sleeping, driving and sleeping, he told me a little about his ex-wife. She'd thrown him out for drugs, of course. And he had a daughter. Mac was in no way under any spell I cast. He wasn't charmed by me or my lovemaking (only once, the first night on the road) or my body or any damn thing about me. I was his ride to his ex-wife, and he made it very clear in just so many words that when we got to New York City, there would be no him and me. I was a bit disappointed to have to sit in the seat of my own car and hear how this gorgeous man was not, definitely not, going to love me; but it was okay, too, because I was, after all, just giving him a ride. A block of time with no man loving me would be a change. "When we get to New York," he told me, looking me right in my Irish eyes, "I'm goin' one way and you're going the other. Do you get me?" he asked.

"I get it," I said, perfectly willing to know the rules of the game. I'd go one way and he'd go the other, without me. I agreed. Basic rules established. But how the heck we'd get there in an old car with bald tires and about twenty dollars between us had yet to be figured out. And I had no idea about the dangers of crossing through Southern states in the mismatched skin colors we were wearing; in spite of his green eyes and latté-colored body, he was Black.

I was asleep when Mac filled up in Gallup, New Mexico, then drove off without paying, in broad daylight—a young Black man with a white teenage girl in an old De Soto with expired Oregon plates. I'd never bothered much with plates before. Steve hadn't bothered to warn or remind me to do something like register the car.

"What's going on?" I asked, raising a sleepy head up from the back seat, which was big enough to be just about comfortable. A funky gas station and dry sprawling desert.

"Stay down," he said. "We're leaving without paying."

"What?" I was surprised. "Won't they just call the cops? It's not like they didn't see you."

It only took about five minutes. We were barely out of Gallup's stretch of last-ditch fill-ups before the sirens came up behind us. The cops chased us briefly, pulled one car in front and another on our side, forcing a stop on the shoulder. Everything looked like dirt and flat land as I watched from the back seat then got out and stood by the car. They put Mac in handcuffs and left me free to go; they didn't even mention the plates, yet.

Mac looked at me little-kid-like as they took him away. Silly. It all seemed so incredibly stupid. I stood by the car in the afternoon sun and breeze in what looked like the middle of nowhere. The officers didn't appear to care how I dealt with all of it. "Where will he be?" I asked. My hair, messed from sleeping, was whipping around in the breeze. I stood by my car in blue jeans and my fringy buckskin jacket, which matched the color of my hair and my eyes when they had nothing green to reflect.

"Gallup City Jail, ma'am," the one shoving Mac into the cop car told me. They said he'd have an arraignment at nine the next morning, and I could bail him out then—and pay for the gas. The officer smiled when he said that.

I figured I had to call someone, so Daddy it was. I could just picture my mature father with the deep voice. I hadn't called home for ages. My mother had said not to drop by, that we didn't have anything to say to each other after that trip to the shrink who said I needed a lot of therapy. My parents hadn't persevered. One little burst of interest, then they cut me off again as if we were total strangers, which, considering the way my siblings and I had been raised, we really were. I'd finally come to realize they needed the extra bedroom enough that considerations for me did not extend past sending me to college. If I was so dumb that I blew that opportunity, it seems, then I was shit outta luck. And for my part, it was pretty easy to act as if they didn't exist. I found a phone booth on a gravelly patch by the side of the road and called home, collect.

 Daddy picked up. I asked for fifty dollars via Western Union to bail out my companion who'd just stolen gas, and he said, "Well, looks to me like you've made your bed and you'll just have to sleep in it. Sorry, can't help." It had been a bit embarrassing to tell him my circumstances, totally too weird for everyone back at the golf-course hacienda. I knew that. I wasn't too surprised, not really. My father was a reasonable man, and I knew that what I was doing and how things were going just wasn't all that reasonable. Nonetheless, I had to raise money. It never occurred to me to just ditch Mac. So I called one of my boyfriends from Reed, the night watchman who was now student body president at Portland State; he'd been a pal ever since I'd successfully used him to get over the onus of virginity. I swore I'd pay him back if he'd trust me. He promised to wire seventy-five bucks to Grants, the closest Western Union office. I headed east with the tank full of stolen gas.

 It had become a gorgeous spring evening, and I could enjoy it without Mac making fun of me for loving nature and beautiful vistas on mother Earth, something drug addicts in withdrawal are totally allergic to, apparently. Sunset on the desert, my elbow resting on the windowsill, cruising along, hair flying in the breeze. Perfect temperature and money coming: fifty for the bail and gas and twenty-five extra bucks to get us on our way. About halfway to Grants, another siren interrupted my reverie, this time directed at me, me alone, and I hadn't done a thing. This was when I learned about the expired plates, and the expired registration in the glove box, and my expired driver's license. I hadn't even looked at any of them. Having prepared myself for an academic career, when it all fell apart in my freshman year, I had zilch in the way of secretarial life skills.

The officer was hefty, a tall Native American. "Aren't you going a little fast?" he asked, leaning into the car, hands on the sill, so we could get a good look at each other. I didn't think I'd been speeding at all. "May I see your license, please, and registration?" I handed over both, and he walked around behind the car and came back. "You'll have to follow me back to the station, Ma'am. You've got an expired registration here, and an expired driver's license, and they don't match."

"Well, it's my ex-boyfriend's car. He did loan it to me," I said, squinting up at him, suddenly aware of how far from home I was.

"But we don't know whether you stole it or not," he said back. I was surprised that someone would accuse me of stealing a car and tried to talk him into letting me go, promising to get it taken care of in the morning, but he wasn't having any of it. So off we went to the local police station in Thoreau, where he locked up the car and turned my keys over to the guys at the little office desk. The impoundment garage also housed a tiny, tinny jail cell.

The short guy in the swivel chair confirmed that I had to spend the night in Thoreau. "We have to do a routine check to see if it's been reported stolen, Ma'am," he explained. If the routine check came back clear at eight a.m., I could go. I argued a bit, insisting on my innocence, but it didn't faze them. I was to spend the night in jail, waiting to be cleared of theft charges.

Mr. Tall Indian Policeman showed me the jail cell that was the saddest place I'd ever seen in my little middle-class life. You know, an old bent piece of tin for a bed, nothing else, a hole in the floor, a light bulb. I must have stared, at this point incredulous that neglecting to reregister Steve's car and forgetting to renew my license would have such harsh results. I made no move to enter the cell that had three painted walls, all monotone off-white, and the stereotypical bars across the front, also painted white. The concrete floor drained to the center, and the metal cot provided the only color with its peeling flesh-beige paint. I couldn't believe that I would really have to sit alone in this room until morning, and on such a nice summer evening. The officer, unlocking the cell door as if it were some kind of funky motel room, ushered me in with a mocking bow. Seeing my dismay, it seemed he felt compassion, and he politely invited me to ride his beat with him instead. He seemed nice, fatherly, and I accepted as if he were doing me a reasonable favor.

The ride around with the officer was fun; I was charmed and amused at the quaint interactions of a small-town cop and his community. From the shotgun front seat, I observed as he stopped and talked to some kids in cars parked off the road just outside of town. I assumed they were drinking, and he made them get in their cars and head home. The laws were fairly loose regarding driving and intoxication in those days. I was simply waiting for the stolen car check to come back negative, so I could be on my way.

Perhaps he knew that someone was going to get me that night and that it may as well be him. Word must've gotten around regarding the gas, the black man, and the girl. I hadn't given any thought to what the townspeople in Gallup might think of us; I was focused on the road and moving toward my next stop—New York City. I also hadn't a clue as to what I'd do upon arriving there, but I was taking it all as it came, one thing at a time. My head full of Kerouac and Steinbeck and those oddballs who lived without plans. Perhaps my insouciance and middle-class ignorance of the world enraged him. I was as oblivious to the officer's world as I was to Mac's. I didn't notice where we were going until I looked out the front window and saw only desert, unfamiliar still, having been in the Southwest just one day. I looked out the other windows, trying not to seem overly alarmed, and saw just desert, too; short, scraggly bushes everywhere, on hard sandy dirt. He had driven out of town quickly, not difficult when town is Thoreau, New Mexico. I had been lulled by the driving around, watching him stop and talk, watching him give a speeding ticket, listening to his cop radio complacently as if he were my daddy and we were out running errands—not that I ever did much of that with my dad, who liked to run errands alone. When I realized we were in the boonies, it hit hard in my belly, like finding out that I'd been dead wrong all along about my gender, or my parents, or something major. Oops. Nothing had ever shaken me quite so deeply. Everything suddenly came into very sharp focus. I envisioned myself, before he even said anything, me, slowpoke me who could only outrun one kid in my gym class—I envisioned a dash into the star-sheltered, head-lighted night; saw myself bolting towards nothingness and sagebrush and imagined the thud and sting of the bullet between my shoulder blades. I guessed he could and might do that if I ran.

He said, "You have to kiss me," as the engine quieted into absolute silence. I said I didn't want to, wishing I could wake up out of the dream, but I had gained at least a second to parlay with him. Besides feeling terror, I was shocked too—a man his age. I'd never really looked at his face much, treating him as a public servant, a high school principal or something, certainly not a man I had for one second considered intimacy with. I don't think that before that moment in my life, that turning point, I viewed all men as potential rapists or lovers.

He had already slid over on the seat and mashed hard up against me before I dared even look his way. It wasn't like I could call for help. There was no help. He was the help. I knew that he towered over me, a huge Navajo, old to me then—unthinkable—maybe thirty-five to my eighteen. Six feet two or three inches, big as my dad, or bigger. The seat beneath my legs was plastic-covered and everywhere there were signs of the law: clipboards, curly phone cords, two-way radio equipment that looked so official. I eyed the door handle and imagined flight again, but dismissed the image of myself dying in the night outside, halfway between Gallup and Grants, New Mexico. I'd heard those two words together so often: rape and murder. I hadn't lived long enough so now I needed a plan, a fast plan. An awareness of my aloneness and a cellular-level assessment that not really very many people would miss me if I didn't show up for breakfast somewhere made me even more desperate to get through whatever was going on. Mac, Mac might miss me, but he'd be easily convinced that I'd just ditched him, disappeared into the sunset.

The officer pressed hard against me and told me I would kiss him: "You have to kiss me." His voice was sickeningly thick as his hand forced my face towards his. His big hands were then all over me, my shoulders and breasts, and I didn't sense any option in the pressure of his grip. I was in a cop car in the middle of nowhere about to get raped or killed or both.

"Okay," I said, and again, slowly, "okay," as if it was something I did every day just to get by, nothing new, "but let's get in back." My gambit was to flatter him (the kissing-up to men we were all so well-trained to do in those days), hoping to gain a little control, some arbitration of the situation, to make him think I liked him even a little. I thought maybe he wouldn't kill me if it seemed like a date, like he was a lover, like it was something other than rape. If I ran and he chased me, I figured there might have been a tussle and dirt and blood and insanity, but fucking in the back seat would mimic something more real, a more familiar experience less likely to end in death. He told me to get out and get in the back seat. He was out his door and around to mine in a second, unzipping and pulling off his holster and gun, which he draped across the open back-seat door. He dropped his pants to his knees and climbed on me as I lay across the seat, my 501s on the floor. There was just a second when I could see him standing there, his massive thighs naked and brown, his shirttails covering his penis. His skin about the same color as Mac's above his black shirt and badge. I wouldn't look at his eyes. He was on me, and I put my arms around him loosely, as if he were my lover. I'd decided my best bet was to give him as much love as I could, and it must have been with those thoughts that the fear went from me and into him. His police-shirt buttons pressed against me, a total stranger, and I thought about loving him like he was any other human I'd held in my arms: the watchman, Randy, Steve, and Mac. The list was four guys long already and I was only eighteen, but the fear had obeyed and left me, apparently pouring into him, and he yelled, jumped back, stood up, pulled up his pants, and started crying into his hands, saying, "Oh my God, I have a wife and kids. What am I doing? Oh my God, what am I doing?" as if I'd seduced him or something, stupid man, and he were some kind of victim. He was really pitiful as he tucked and zipped but it was my advantage. Sweet Jesus, it was my victory.

What a relief to be still breathing, no underwear wrapped around my neck to force the air out of me so I couldn't tell, and as he cried and buckled I pulled my clothes back on calmly, eyes down, as if it hadn't really been so bad, as if it hadn't really happened at all, I knew I was still in danger, not safe yet. I had no idea it would be decades before I felt safe again. We didn't speak for a few minutes as he turned his black-and-white cop car around, and we headed back to town.

As soon as there were gas stations and buildings in view, I asked him for my keys. I'd seen him pocket them. "I think you should give me my car keys now and let me go when we get back," I said, knowing I had to say something. There were at least two more cops in the station, and it was late in the night. I wanted to find us both a way out of the situation by asking for my keys and car rather than discussing any other options such as reporting him, which of course might have resulted in him trying to silence me. I sounded in charge even to myself, as much as I could keep my voice steady, feeling the life I'd come from of Buicks and summers of thin cotton dresses, cleaning the big house for my mother, feeling the privileged, middle-class power I hoped I had in me. He dug in his pocket and handed me the keys. My request had implied I wouldn't tell if he'd just let me go. I wanted him to trust me not to tell, to let me get the hell out of there and drive away from him and his pig friends.

There was another test to pass when I stood at the desk in the station with the dark, quiet night at my back; the only light for miles was the glaring overhead bulb in the small office space behind the counter. The attached garage that contained my car was dark. The jail cells were through a hall behind a closed door and issued no sound. The two pairs of eyes looking back at me were neither cheering nor light-filled. They were defending the peace in Thoreau, and I was the only criminal around. Officer Tall Indian Man stood behind me, waiting for them to give me release papers of some sort—something to show that I'd been cleared, that there was no all-state alert for an old De Soto with a teenage girl at the wheel.

I was sure, still, that my voice had to carry authority or the thin line between life and death might yet be crossed by one of the men in the office. As I spoke I sensed all of them making up their own versions of how the story might go. The energy in the garage-office wasn't that hard to read: maybe they took turns raping lone female travelers. It was three in the morning. It didn't occur to me until many decades had passed, that the rape was a hate crime. The racism hadn't really sunk in that a white, teenaged girl traveling through Indian lands with a Black man might be enraging to a racist. The officer's desire to hurt and humiliate me had to do with his low opinion of me. I announced to them that I was leaving early because the officer had told me it was okay, dangling my keys to prove it, but not provocatively, nothing smug—I called up a poker face I must have learned in lying to my mother, who most certainly preferred lies to truth. Truth just caused her too much grief. The truth I had to hide from these men was my anger. I had to pretend to be alright. I had to pretend I wasn't hurt and humiliated.

"He said I could go now." Listening to myself, I sounded steady and calm. I looked at the one seated facing me. He skipped a beat taking a long look at me, then nodded to the one beside him. There was the pause, but no one asked for an explanation. Short guy at the swivel chair scooted over to the teletype machine and officially verified that my clearance had indeed just come through; he solemnly passed me a warning to get the other paperwork up to date. They switched on the lights in the garage behind us, opened the doors, and I left without another word. By the time I got the money in Grants and drove back to the courthouse in Gallup, there was barely time for a short nap. Mac didn't show much feeling one way or the other when I paid his bail. We headed east again.

He did abandon me our first morning in Manhattan. My car was parked on Canal Street about five blown tires and dozens of hours and days of panhandling for gas and retreads later. Surely we had angels protecting us during those terrifying blowouts. He said good-bye, made a sweep of my green eyes with his, then just got out and walked away, looking like a magazine model, a scant smile crossing his face.

"I'm splitting, you know," he said, "and you're not coming with me." I didn't really need to be told twice. No pity for me or from me, but I could see a second of recognition passing in his selfish, drug-addict mind: recognition of abandonment. But there were no rules other than the moment and I wasn't afraid, just curious about how it would all turn out. Mac was headed toward his ex-wife's house, and it would not do to have me come along. He knew I was clueless about life, and he wasn't looking for a job as my instructor.

I locked the car and walked to the nearest park, which happened to be Washington Square, and met a couple of guys right away who offered to let me sleep at their places. I moved around. Hung out. I walked around, just walked and walked and walked every day, talked to people who would talk, and panhandled for meals. As I was jobless and without resources, no one wanted much to do with me. I loaned out my car to some kids who wrecked it and stole my sleeping bag, which I had stupidly left in the trunk, unlocked—still a naive Oregon girl.

One of my guy friends was trying to get me a job in a coffeehouse where he worked, suggesting that a job might improve my situation, and it was hard to disagree with that. But it got old, panhandling for food. I didn't know why I was in New York, or why I was anywhere exactly. I got the clap and had a very bad reaction to penicillin; this scared me, kind of blew my fledgling confidence, collapsing at the hospital, being rushed into the ER on a stretcher covered in huge water blisters. I called my dad and claimed I was very sick and asked for a ticket home to Eugene on my nineteenth birthday, June of 1965, to try the whole thing over, one more time. I have recently considered that if I'd had no one to bail me out back then, I would've been forced to grow up—get that job, clear my head of fog and futility and get on with creating a life for myself. But that wasn't my path. I had a family and I returned, a prodigal daughter, at least temporarily. No wonder they disowned me about a year later. If they were alive now, I'd thank them for that.

My parents met me at the airport, and I sat in back with the two little kids, numbers four and five, for whom I'd changed diapers and to whom I'd spoon-fed pabulum and applesauce for several years each. These two were like strangers to me, and my mother, as distant as ever, was showing me mostly the back of her head. My dad spoke coolly, remotely, about how I looked pretty good and didn't look sick to him.

I wanted somehow to have a plan back then at their ranch-style house in the suburbs, a normal pattern and sequence of events, and for the duration of the summer, they tolerated me being a kid again, and I tolerated them being distant and judgmental. I worked and went to summer school, but it didn't take. I couldn't make the straight life stick. Mom threw a fit and called me promiscuous and a slut (nasty word) for sleeping with my boyfriend Randy who had just graduated high school. She screamed at me for not wanting to marry him, (even though I'm married to him now) and that was that. Making A's at the U of Oregon and holding a job at the A&W drive-in didn't offset whatever she feared regarding my sex life. What? That I was enjoying myself, my young body and healthy good looks? I was out the window at midnight when Steve came through town, wooing me again. Summer school had ended, and I hopped into the back of the pickup headed to the Red Dog Saloon in Virginia City, Nevada, on the road again. Randy was on the back burner.

Merimée Moffitt

The Red Dog Saloon

We were outsiders even in the Wild West town of Virginia City, Nevada. Everyone else was American or tourist; we were counter culture and raw, let our raggedy edges show: chewed up by families, marriages, wars, drugs, impossible standards of living. The sheriff of VC came to Greta's pad where we'd been crashing for a few days and offered us a house—all we had to do was clean out the trash, the nested rodents, the desert which had moved in through glass-less windows and bent doors. He took us in his car to see the two little houses he said we could live in for free, and though the six-inch deep crap and debris in the main house was disheartening, the little handmade stone cabin in the side yard was a score. Paul and Barefoot John Hendricks were happy enough with the four room rodents' nest. They had it looking good enough to call home in just a couple of days.

Steve and I claimed the Stone House, as it was one tiny, slightly L-shaped room, and who could argue with squatters' rights? It sat high on the driveway looking out at desert rock formations. An abandoned gold mine just down the steep incline. So sunny, so quiet, I was enchanted. We'd have to get a six foot expanse of glass to set in the unfinished, grey wood frame, good enough still to hold the window. I loved the sunken bathtub which I guessed had never, nor would it ever while we were there, see water. I didn't even try to picture us settling in for the long cold winter. We were end of summer visitors only. With nothing, not a penny nor a vehicle, no jobs during the off-season, we'd have to flee like everyone else. An iron bed and mattress materialized. The skylight strangely had unbroken glass. The original builders had been so close to finishing their little dream cabin. The walls consisted of hand-set, cantaloupe-sized grey stones entirely, all around, with a poured concrete floor.

    The picture window glass made it all the way from Carson City in Nick's old Caddy convertible until it cracked as it sat leaning on the stone wall, just seconds from being set in and puttied. It didn't bother me, yet Steve was livid with self-loathing and universal rage; I reasoned with him that the two pieces fit together anyway. We'd glue it or something. The house would be cold as the arctic, and we'd have to vacate anyway. I didn't mind the crack. Everything was like that then: imperfect, half-done, stuck together as best as possible. That's how we'd become too. Clinging, almost connected, fitting like puzzle pieces to keep out the worst of the worst demons and coldness. We spent some lovely afternoons, a few cold nights huddling, snuggling, sleeping, screwing on that skinny bed under the fit-together window.

The view looked out on Nevada hills, dotted with shrubby trees, roads lined with poppies the Chinese workers had planted for their relaxation times. Not a building or sign of humanity in sight. Gold Hill, two miles down the mountain from Virginia City, had nothing in 1965: maybe one bar and two houses, maybe, but we never had money to go into the bar. The place was a ghost town, and I loved it enough for a while.

We spent about a month surviving there on tips and an occasional meal for the jug band at the Red Dog, whatever I made from Jenna, babysitting. I had worked for Jenna the cook as sous chef briefly until she moved me down to her house to watch her kids while she worked. Nick had been her childcare-giver until all the band members showed up and the P. H. Phactor jug band from Seattle was reborn: Nick, lead guitar, mouth harp and crooner; John Browne, rhythm guitar and singer; John Hendricks, mandolin and occasional banjo; Paul, rhythm washboard with brass on his fingertips; and Steve, jug player, bass guitar, singer, and owner of the thick long blonde hair and Nordic god good looks, and Merimee, babysitter to the cook, ace pie maker.

We took some day trips to hot springs, night trips just walking back down the mountain to Gold Hill where our free house clung to the side of scraggly desert dirt and rock. The sheriff had befriended us and I felt safe. I rarely considered danger in those days. Those were still the days before people started locking everything up.

Dan Hicks and his Hot Licks played that summer; Janis and Big Brother had been there before we got there. Lynn Hughes the Queen of the Blues was the house singer and hostess. It was fairy-tale like. Then the owner, Mark, announced the last call: he'd be closing in a few weeks for the winter, and people started scattering in various directions.

Steve left me to wait for a postcard from him while he looked for farm work in the Sacramento Valley. It didn't take long. He sent me bus money and met me just outside of Arbuckle where the bus stopped at a dusty intersection. He was with some sweet thing who had a car and a trailer he'd stayed in while job hunting. There was energy between them, and I wasn't sure if he would really choose me over her. We hitched away from her, however, to another chapter of our saga.

He'd had been hired on a sugar beet farm to cull the last beets out of the rows, the big ones stuck too deep, escapee beets from the harvester's claws, or lone football-sized sugar beets, which had over shot the dump truck. The farmer wanted them all to go to market, and Steve's job was to put the dump truck in compound low and run alongside with his curved beet knife, a scythe, swooping down and scooping up and flinging all the leftover tubers into the truck bed all freaking day long. We never thought about being tired back then. I was so bored sitting around the big old farmhouse, I'd go out to the fields and help stab and toss the beets high up over the edge of the dump truck. We'd do that until the dang truck—an entire dump truck was filled up. Then he, or rather we, would drive them to the train station and unload into a car that would take them to the factory.

The fields seemed miles across; the edges of the property almost too far to see, and every day was sunny and dry.

When we were shown our quarters in the old mansion, I was thrilled. The house was two story, set in an oasis of yards and old trees. Two Mexicans lived upstairs the boss said, as he showed us around; we'd be the only ones on the first floor which had two bedrooms, an old farm-house kitchen, a dining room, an empty living room. The ceilings were high with ornate moldings, the kitchen floor the original linoleum, old oak everywhere else. A few objects were left so the place was habitable for transient farmhands, or maybe it just hadn't been picked clean yet. We chose a tiny bedroom off the kitchen, but the other bedroom, the one off the dining room, had an amazing stash of vintage clothing—originals which no one in the family had bothered to move. I knew I'd spend a great deal of time pawing through them. There also was a little concertina in another closet, and when I started complaining of absolute boredom, Steve attempted to show me some tunes. But my malaise was deep and mysterious to me. While he worked dawn to dark, I, wifey-poo fixing lunch and dinner, tried to be a songbird. But I hadn't had a lick of musical education like he had, and I just couldn't care long enough to learn. I liked to be sung to; performing was entirely a different deal. I had liked singing and playing my guitar while still at home, but we'd pawned the guitar and Steve said I wasn't much of a singer. All I needed, in retrospect, was some encouragement—what a huge loss of opportunity I couldn't see then. He, for some reason, didn't want me singing.

Within a few days of learning how to fling the random beets into the truck bed he taught me how to shift through the eighteen gears and how to slow down for curves and stop lights. I loved it but only got in one run to the train before I was tattled on. The guys at the dump site knew something was amiss when I got out of the driver's side after negotiating the ramp and put the truck in place to dump into the train car. I did it perfectly, but I was a girl. The phones must've been ringing at the ranch house about who was hiring "girl" drivers—unheard off in 1965. Women were not allowed to do men's work—period. The next day, as we were both running along and flinging beets—hey, I was working for free!—Farmer John roared up in his truck, stomped over to us, and announced that if Steve wanted the job, he had to keep me where I belonged—in the house.

I grumbled a bit but did what I was told, and that led to really exploring the old mansion. I investigated an old cook shack attached to the side of the kitchen, functioning back when there were dozens of men to do what the big machines were built to do, and women to cook for them quite possibly, on the outdoor woodstove, under a roof with the sides all screened in. I loved it: several long wooden tables with benches and a big-bellied wood cook stove that was still adorned with nearby racks of dangling cast iron pans. Inside. I snooped through the Mexican workers' apartment upstairs. Their tortilla press sitting in a pile of masa dust was interesting. I'd never seen masa or a tortilla press, or the mess left on a small table after these farm hands had made themselves some breakfast with the special tortillas.

It didn't take me long to get abysmally bored. It seemed there was no place on this planet for me, specifically. What women were supposed to do just didn't mean shit to me—cooking, cleaning, shining themselves up to pander to their mate's appetites just made me want to die inside. I'd get comatose, depressed they call it now, or bi-polar, or borderline, or schizoid. I was simply too aware of all that I couldn't do in a man's world, and completely at a loss at what I might actually like to do with my life. I didn't blame anyone. I didn't feel angry; I was just bored stiff and lacking resources to look beyond that door, that farm with my gorgeous friend busy working to get us car money. It seemed to me I'd tried everything there was to try and I hated it all. I didn't regret climbing out the window of the bedroom my parents had let me use just a couple of months back, didn't regret blowing off college—not then anyway. I was still too young and dumb to know what I'd lost in following Steve around as his personal assistant aka whore, cook, companion. And he was clueless—and why would he want to direct me towards my own life, my own power? I was like a dog he loved, but he wasn't my dog; I could cook and was willing to fuck and do whatever he wanted—wash his clothes, shop, make his bed—but it all got me really down. I'd run out of books. I could have loved him more and better if I'd known then to get my own life, but to get my own life was a foreign idea. I hadn't ever thought that thought. Neither of us could figure out the dots to connect to make me feel whole and excited. I was simply his woman; I tagged along; seriously not enough challenge or focus for me, but I wasn't aware of it, still following the model of so much male literature.

What women had to say in their small establishment, at that time, of women writers, would be something I'd turn to eventually—but it hadn't occurred to me yet. I had no idea how to find women writers, how to get my hands on their books, but I was working up to it. I was not ahead of my time in buying into the oppression of women. But I at least indulged in sheer willfulness; I couldn't be compliant forever, not for long, not eternally. In the rancher's house, I simply would shut down and stay in bed or on bed and stare and wait. I had nowhere I wanted to go, but I did like the dresses and the history of the place, and after the rancher's inevitable assault on me, I paid myself with a few of the treasures long dusty and unappreciated.

I'd been in the bedroom trying on the most astonishing of the evening gowns and afternoon dresses that must've belonged to his mother, aunts, grandmother, and even one from the turn of the century that was to die for. This one I would definitely steal on pay day, just for his arrogant negativity in firing me from working for free. It fit beautifully—soft, slightly shimmering lavender velvet with cream-colored lace, full length, 1920's era. A bit matronly but gorgeous with pearls sewn in dripping patterns around the hips, sheer chiffon on the shoulders—a work of art. This kind of woman stuff I appreciated. What happened that day, next, isn't such a biggie, but the absolute flatness of the energy in the house and the job, made it a memorable event. I was in my own clothes, my burgundy gabardine man shirt over jeans, when he sauntered in behind me talking about the dresses and grabbing me simultaneously. He'd told me I could have them all if I'd just do a little something for him as he put me in a neck lock with one arm and one hand up my shirt on my naked breast with the other, and I was pissed off and sickened, surprising myself that my "No" was quite energetic. I didn't feel like he'd kill me as there were too many workers around who might, not likely, but might have noticed his truck pulled up to the house. My back was to the open bedroom door; I'd arranged a pile of dresses spread around the bed as if dozens of women were coming to try them on, and yes, I loved the dresses, but I wasn't about to trade sex for them with this obnoxious and desperate idiot. We tussled a little, and I knew I had to get us both, locked in the struggle, out of that room if I stood a chance. First, just shaking him away as if that might work, then "No, just leave me alone" loud, really loud, pushing him and his arms off me with every ounce of strength I had. By that time we were in the old dining room which had deep sash windows, where the curtains were open to the fields; he re-set his hat and stomped out of the room hard on his cowboy boot heels without another word. We'd already been there about a month, and I knew we needed two or three more weeks to get money for a car. Poor creepy man. How can guys live with that kind of hateful energy?

I didn't want to make a huge deal out of it because he did, after all, let me go, but I was too shaken up not to tell Steve, who jumped up from the lunch I had set out on the kitchen table and said he was going to kill the son-of-a-bitch, but I trotted after him saying "No, no, it wasn't that bad." I didn't want any Wild West killing going on—too dangerous and besides, the farmer could just off the two of us and who would ever know? Who would have even missed us? No one knew where we were or cared. Mr. Crazy Rapist Rancher/Farmer was right outside where the machinery was left at lunch. I stood behind Steve, but close. It was a bright, warm day, and the other workers were distant but watching. The boss listened to Steve telling him, "Hey Man, don't be coming in the house, and keep your goddamned hands off my girlfriend," leaning into the guy but not going after him. Steve was a formidable character, threatening enough that the older dude surely didn't want a fistfight.

The farmer said, "Yeah, well you keep her outta my trucks (as if we didn't know that already, but it was a bargaining point), and come pay day the two of you can hit the road." We had essentially been fired, but it didn't matter. We had enough to make it.

That pay day we hitched to Arbuckle, the closest town, and bought a cheap little Chevy coupe that would at least get us to the City. The next morning, a Saturday, we left before dawn with a few dresses, a mirror, and a 10" cast iron pan from the cook shack that I still use almost every day. Still! I was nervous that he'd be at the end of the driveway and not let us leave with the dresses and the pan and the mirror, but he didn't bother, and I was grateful. It was just a few hours to San Francisco and John Browne's house in the Haight. To this day, I have no idea how Steve always knew where his friends were. People not only didn't have cell phones, but most of us lived without landlines, too. Musicians had a way of knowing where everyone was.

Dining in the Haight

The only clock was on the kitchen stove—no phone, no radio or TV anywhere in the apartment. The guys owned instruments; I owned a portable Singer sewing machine. The washboard player occupied the attic as a bedroom. John, folk-singing heart throb of the Portland coffee house scene, had found the place and rented it after his old lady in Portland dumped him and he moved to San Francisco. Steve and I moved in after the beet farm in Arbuckle even though John said he didn't really want to share his two-bedroom apartment. I heard him tell Steve he was getting over Lena, the one who'd dumped him and squished his heart like a cigarette butt on a sidewalk. He wanted to live alone. "I've got a job," he said. "I can pay rent. I don't need roommates." But we put our bedroll in his extra room, and by the time Nick, Hendricks, and Bassett arrived, John (considered today the best folk guitarist in the Pacific Northwest, Vashon Island) was caught up in the idea of being second guitar and singer in the P. H. Phactor. John's apartment had an attic which no one else in the building was using: windows on each end, eaves on both sides, little areas divided by the old chimneys, and a complete pine board floor. Perfect! We all helped John with the rent and shared the kitchen; I'd often cook enough soup or rice or spaghetti for multitudes.

Every morning was a new beginning, but I didn't expect great surprises. There wouldn't be food besides grain, maybe enough money for two muffins from the bakery on Haight Street, maybe enough for oatmeal and milk if Steve had made good tips the night before at the Matrix, the bar in North Beach that seemed to appreciate the jug band's music. The free beer and peanuts from the bar was often dinner but I didn't mind that, in fact, of course, I loved to wake up hungry. At home, I'd always tried so hard to be hungry, skipping days of Mother's cooking, swishing a few bits of Rice Krispies and a spoon of milk in a bowl so it looked like I'd eaten breakfast. Here it was a piece of cake, so to speak.

We awoke that day, as usual, in a rumple of white sheets and sunshine, naked, relaxed. I could do whatever I wanted, every day. We were totally broke, but I didn't want a real job right then. The band pulled in enough to make rent and utilities, sort of. I earned a little on my sewing machine—hems and patches and buttons mostly. "I'll make some tea and oatmeal," I told Steve.

"We're jamming at the Dead's today," he said, rolling over in bed and folding his arms behind his head so he could watch me get dressed. I liked how he watched me; assessing my softness and strong bones as I struggled into beige jeans from the Goodwill that were undeniably too tight, stretching on tip toe to tug the zipper up. I didn't like too tight jeans as they gave me a roll of fat over the waistline, but with Goodwill clothes sometimes close enough had to do. He smiled his golden-boy grin. Then a white cotton blouse, the Mexican peasant kind that didn't need underwear, pulled down over naked breasts. That was it; two articles of clothing. There was no mirror in the room, and I avoided the one in the bathroom; I didn't like mirrors. The gilt-framed artifact stolen from the rancher may have still been in the attic; I didn't attach to it. I instinctively didn't want to live with what I looked like to others as a dominant concern, even though the depth and depravity of the beauty culture was a far larger battle than I could articulate at the time. My parents seemed to think my role in life was to be attractive to every single man on the planet so that eventually, one would offer me a job as his personal, full-time whore/slave. It was my upbringing, to be concerned how I looked every second of every day. Living without mirrors was an effort, albeit unconscious, to know my internal worth, my self. The flame was feeble, but it would be a thread of sparks for me to follow in the dark, to my own value. A brush through thick brown hair and letting it fall was sufficient. In truth, I knew I had beautiful hair, and a washing and brushing was all it needed.

"Okay," I answered him. "All afternoon?"

"Yeah," he replied, "a few hours probably. They want to learn our 'New Minglewood Blues,' and tomorrow we're moving some of their big stuff down to the new house." He rolled over like he planned to sleep while I fixed food.

The large square kitchen was the only room in the apartment that felt like it was primarily mine—what a surprise. The floor was gritty as usual but the feel of careless housekeeping was better than fighting reality—too many people always cruising through just getting it dirty again. The long, old-fashioned counter held a gallon jar of short-grain brown rice, Chico San, which I bought by the fifty-pound sack at the turn-of-the-century dry-goods-turned-health-food store in the Mission district. Oatmeal it would be this morning, with raisins and brown sugar and there was, amazingly, some milk in the empty fridge.

"Hey, I put honey in this tea. Do you want some?" I held the steaming brew under Steve's nose, and he woke up agreeably for his breakfast, taking the tea and setting it on the floor by the bed. I put the bowl beside it. He ran his fingers through his mane of shoulder-length, dishwater blonde hair, then tossed it back and sat up cross legged under the white sheet, his tablecloth.

My dark-red leather steamer trunk held most of my possessions—it hadn't come with us from the beet farm. I found it in a Goodwill or on the street, and it was fast filling with scores from thrift shops all over the Filmore, the Mission, the Haight-Ashbury. Not many people knew or cared about vintage clothing in those days. The trend to dress in your grandmother's style was new and hugely possible in San Francisco. We were setting trends then, out of necessity and common sense. I already had to get out of the tight jeans, just not a tight jeans day, so I pulled out a slightly wrinkled, rayon dress and wiggled it down over my again-naked body. Steve's physique sitting cross-legged made him look like a longhaired Adonis in the lotus position. I smoothed the dress over my naturally rounded belly and hips and zipped the little dress zipper, which like lots of forties dresses, was under my arm on the left side. On the bed, I pulled on cowboy boots, soft, well-worn Justins with a suede bottom and smooth, natural leather tops. "I'm going down to Chuck and Blythe's," I told him. I liked getting out and stretching in the morning with a brisk walk. It was spring in the city and I felt like walking, visiting, seeing what was out there. "So I'll see you sometime later today?" I asked him, lying back onto the low bed (plywood on concrete blocks with a foam pad, white sheets, pale wool blanket from God knows where). Steve and I were more like sibling puppies than adult lovers. I liked to touch and tussle, be held, scrap around, which usually ended up with him on top of me and fast and furious fucking. I nudged his hip with my head, looked up at his tanned torso from that angle—he was gorgeous from any view point. He finished by drinking the milk from the bottom of the bowl.

"Yeah," he replied, hopping up and grabbing his blue jeans. I watched him button up after stuffing in the tails of a striped cotton shirt. Everything fit him so easily. He always was the perfect weight, no matter what he did to himself. "I'm helping them set up for a high school dance in Marin tonight. You wanna go with us?" he asked on his way out the door.

"Yeah, that sounds fun." I was used to being invited along and liked it; it was what I did, tag along behind this guy. Crossing the Golden Gate Bridge even if it was just to lug instruments and cords and speakers into the school gym for the Grateful Dead's high school graduation gig sounded like a good destination for an afternoon. The Dead lived one block over, same distance uphill from Haight Street as our apartment.

"Okay, we'll come by and get you," and he was gone. I lay under the round tri-colored glass window he'd ripped off from some open building, trying to please me, and maybe even just keeping up with the Joneses as every hippie household became denser and richer with street scores, old construction items, posters from the concerts that were starting to happen regularly: stuff. But I didn't like that it was red, white and blue; or that he'd stolen it.

I hadn't seen Blythe for ages, and the thought energized me. I grabbed Steve's abandoned dishes to drop them in the sink, then headed out to the stairs and the street level front door of the big old house which, like most of the houses above Haight Street, was an old Victorian now divided into flats and apartments.

The hill was steep but walking down the broad sidewalk in the bright San Francisco morning felt great. My friends' apartment was just a few blocks down and around the corner, in the basement of a shady old house that faced the Panhandle section of the Golden Gate Park.

Chuck, a small, dark-haired poet and, like Gary Snyder, a former Northwest logger, opened the door to his basement pad, happy to see me as usual and invited me in with a nod and a sweep of his arm. "Blythe's getting the baby to go to sleep," he said, as he walked over to his work table and sat on a high stool, picking up a tobacco pouch. He was just about my height, maybe shorter when I wore my boots. I didn't feel nervous around Chuck. He was a poet and kind to living creatures, and married. I could hear the two older kids playing in the bathtub shrieking and splashing and figured they'd be out in the living room jumping all over me and asking funny questions as soon as they got dressed. I plunked down on the old fuzzy sofa to just sit and think about things, then realized there was another adult in the front rooms of the tiny apartment.

From my position on the couch, I had a good view through the doorway of the man in the next room who seemed to be digging in the kitchen trash can with unusual absorption. I could see he was tall, even bent over like he was, squatting with his back to us, and that he had a lot of hair. "Who is that?" I asked Chuck, who avoided straight jobs and was currently learning to work with brass and beads. Chuck and Blythe were artists and parents and always had something going on, always something to see or eat or smoke or talk about. Today it was the big guy in a blanket going through their garbage can.

"That's Christian Larsen," Chuck answered. "You don't know Christian?"

"No, I've never seen him before." The man was standing now, picking around on some food on a plate.

"He's been around forever," Chuck continued. "I can't believe you've never met him." Chuck and his family lived on the fringe of the fringe, true fringies—right now selling the brass jewelry and mobiles they made at home. Blythe did beadwork on clothes and moccasins and sometimes made French pastries for coffee houses. Chuck was rolling himself a cigarette from a blue Bugler bag when his son and daughter came tearing through the room in underpants, chasing each other like kittens. They romped across the sofa and my lap just as I'd guessed they would, but I loved to have them frolic all over with their strong little bodies. The long-haired boy was about five and was laughing at his younger sister as she tried to catch him. They headed into the bedroom and came right back out with their mother on their heels, her hands full of clothing.

She herded the children back into the bedroom to make them finish dressing. Blythe gave one of her beautiful smiles and nodded for me to follow, but I stayed in the front room to find out more about the strange man.

"Well, what's he doing going through your garbage?" By that time Christian had filled his plate completely with stuff from the pail at the end of the kitchen counter and was standing a full six foot six, eating with his fingers, seemingly absorbed in the taste of whatever he'd found in the trash. He had wild, shoulder-length red hair and a wiry reddish beard that reached almost to his waist. A rope was wrapped a couple of times around a thick woolen serape that added to the impression of massiveness. I rolled myself a Bugler and lit up with a stick match from Chuck's jewelry table, noticing Christian's raggedy sleeves and pants.

"Why do you eat garbage?" I asked from my position back on the sofa, one leg swinging over the other, not worried at all about offending him and not really wanting to squeeze into the tiny bedroom with Blythe and her kids. I glanced at my own bare calves showing above the cowboy boots. I liked the swell of muscle that seemed just right, a pleasing compliment to the curve of my boot top. Christian, still standing in the doorway, finished his last bite and wiped the back of his hand across his lips, then across his hip.

"I don't like to see things go to waste," he said, "and I've never seen a garbage can yet that didn't have a meal in it." He had a rasping, deep voice and looked about thirty, and a lot of that time spent outside. He turned back into the kitchen to put the plate away. Blythe was now shuttling the two kids out of the back rooms and through the door that opened onto a small courtyard. She would be opening the sandbox for them to enjoy while it was sunny out, and she'd probably stay out there with them working on something while they played and the baby slept inside.

"You mean you don't have to cook or shop? You just go around eating people's garbage?" He had a good line but I didn't really believe him, that he could be that pure. "What if you can't find anything and you get hungry?"

He said he'd been eating this way for years and hadn't starved yet. "As a matter of fact, I don't get too hungry and I don't get sick," he said with just a bit of an accent. Certainly Nordic or Scandinavian parents. Christian moved into the tiny living room and seated himself on a low stool, having set his plate on the counter in the kitchen, rinsed and dried like a good boy.

Chuck was sitting at his work table, fiddling with some wire and beads, but he turned and introduced us properly: "Merimee, Christian; Christian, Merimee. Hey, how come you two didn't run into each other before in Seattle? I know we were all there at the same time."

"I almost never left the house that winter," I remember telling Chuck, remembering also the long cold winter of rain and snow and Steve's absence when he attempted to go south to Mexico to score kilos, but returned empty-handed. "God, I probably only met about five people in my five months in Seattle." I wanted to go outside and visit with Blythe, but I was fascinated by Christian's sandals. He was unwrapping a length of twine that held what looked like three layers of tire tread to his feet. The treads were stitched together with baling wire, and the twine worked like long laces holding leather straps that came from between the two bottom layers. These were the original, the first tire-tread shoes I'd ever seen, and they seemed to work pretty well as homemade shoes.

"Now, that's a good idea," I commented, noticing also the darning maintenance on his thick wool socks. I liked to make stuff on my sewing machine like pullover dresses with elastic here and there instead of zippers and darts and plackets and yokes. My mother had taught me to sew the spring before I left home for Reed; good thing too, as sewing became a way of supporting myself more than once. I liked using remnants, old curtains, fabrics from other decades to make unique and free clothing, which sometimes I wore, sometimes I sold. I could relate to Christian's ways of survival: take something discarded and make useful stuff out of it, especially shoes. "I bet those are really comfortable too. Did you make them?" I imagined how bouncy three layers of tire tread might be, compared to the hard leather of cowboy boots on San Francisco's sidewalks.

"Yes, I made these," he answered. "I don't see any reason to buy shoes." His voice sounded remote like he didn't do lots of talking with anyone. His carefully chosen words came out a little slowly.

"So you just slap on another sole when one gets worn out?" I asked, wondering just how tall he would be with five or six layers of tread on his sandals. He had one of the shoes in his hands now, tugging on the wires that had come loose. His fingers looked tough and weathered and not-so-clean. I wished they were cleaner so I could love the guy a little more.

"Well, I think they're really neat shoes. But I'll tell you," I said, changing the subject back to food, "there's no way you'd ever find a meal in my kitchen garbage." Between me and Steve and the guys in the attic, there wasn't any food left over or around or anything. The fridge looked more like Old Mother Hubbard's cupboard than a place to store perishables. I could picture an onion quarter, dried and yellowed, maybe some French's mustard. It was a bleak picture, like a room after everyone's moved out with the light shining into empty corners, dust in the places where things had sat too long. I tried to picture any edibles in my kitchen trash and only summoned up a gob of burned short grain brown rice and some avocado peels. I also knew that any mention of his checking out my garbage was a bit flirtatious, but I craved conversation. I really did hope Christian would be a good guy with a few words of wisdom, stories, memorized poems—anything.

"I never throw anything away except maybe a little rice if I burn it," I told him. "But I don't see how you could make a meal out of that."

"Well, I'd like to come by your place sometime just to see what I find," he countered, slowly, looking like pictures of Walt Whitman I'd seen in high school. I told him where we lived, on the corner of Clayton and Frederick. Maybe he really was an elevated guy, and we'd talk about something interesting: books or friendship, or where to find the best apples, or walking across the United States.

I got up quickly, saying, "Bye, gotta go now, but I'm gonna find Blythe first." I gave Christian vague directions to the apartment over my shoulder, felt him checking out my curvy body under the softly draping dress patterned in tiny pansies, but didn't care much if he looked. I liked the way my hips felt moving under the slinky skirt, my stride long and strong in boots. Braless and feeling good in natural fabric was my thing, and just too bad for the guys if they were disturbed by unbound breasts.

I saw trouble on Blythe's face the minute I stepped outside, as if she'd been crying off and on for days. The two children were engrossed with filling small containers in a sandbox in the corner of the courtyard which had high concrete walls, mostly ivy covered. Blythe sat on the bench of an old and graying picnic table, her beading basket on the table but her hands listless in her lap. "What is it?" I asked surprised, having never seen this friend so in the dumps before.

"Oh, it's Chuck," she said, pulling more Kleenex out of her dress pocket. She had on a cotton fifties' dress that had two handy pockets sewn on the front for household items: clothespins, diaper pins, the whatevers of housewifery—big pockets with ruffles across the tops. Blythe was taking her time with an answer.

"What?" I insisted, seating myself on the bench in the twinkly, almost warm San Francisco sun. "What is it?" I was thinking maybe he had a disease or something, but Blythe was shaking her head and looking genuinely sad. Her auburn hair fell forward over both shoulders. I always thought she had the prettiest full lips, the only ones I'd ever seen that looked really good in dark red lipstick.

"He keeps disappearing and not explaining, and, finally, yesterday, he told me he's been having an affair." She spoke hesitantly, as if not wanting to tell, but too desperate not to.

"Oh my God," I said, quite aware that Blythe needed her husband to help feed the three kids. "What are you going to do?"

"Nothing," she answered, looking down at her lap. "What can I do? But I told him he had to stop, and he said he would."

I felt angry at Chuck but understood when Blythe told me who it was. Natalie Carmagnani was awesomely beautiful: slim-hipped, full-breasted, tall and graceful. She wore red silk like nobody else could, her elegant, creamy-white Italian skin enviable against her mane of shiny black hair. Some of us knew Natalie's musician old man put bruises on that soft skin, sometimes hard-to-hide ones on her face. Natalie's beauty was dazzling, no doubt about it. I thought Chuck must have been flattered that she had chosen him.

"God," I said to Blythe, "it must be an ego thing."

Blythe could only nod her head.

"He won't stay with her," I ventured, pretty sure he

really wouldn't. Besides, very unlikely Natalie would keep him on. "He's too good, Blythe. He won't leave you."

We sat and watched the children play for a minute. When I went back through the living room, Chuck and Christian were gone.

My boots clomped the few blocks back home to the apartment in bright, late-morning sun, crossing Haight Street at the light, and then up the hill on the wide dirty-white sidewalk dotted with smashed gum and litter. Aluminum garbage cans sat in the corners behind the stoops of many of the old apartment buildings; some were tucked under jutting-out bay windows; some even sat on the sidewalk at the end of very short driveways. I wondered if Christian rummaged through these cans, too, or if he just did private kitchens.

I got home in time to catch the ride over the Bay in the late afternoon with Phil Lesch and Steve. We didn't stay for the gig, a high school graduation dance; it was just friendly and fun to go to Marin to help them haul and set up their new electric equipment; they were mentors to the jug band—they'd been a jug band too before going electric with Owsley's financial help. I guess Owsley admired them and wanted to float his LSD into their concerts in cahoots with their psychedelic music—he had to do something with his drug money, and he needed some broad distribution. The Dead were pretty good advertisers for the mind-altering tripping acid so it all wove together. Phil and even Jerry himself used to stand at the doorway of some of their first concerts and hand it out as paying customers streamed into the Avalon or wherever.

When I heard the knock on the door the next day, I knew all the way down the hall that it was Christian. Everyone else who came and went—including the little thieves from the neighborhood I'd caught digging through my dresser drawers—everyone we knew just walked in. Before opening the door, I felt a surge of regret that I'd given myself the task of dealing with this strange man.

"Well, hello, come on in." I greeted him cordially, nervous because I was in my own place now and had more or less invited him over. I hoped it wouldn't become an ordeal, that he really would be more Walt-like than Jack the Ripper-esque. I stood aside in the narrow entry hall, signaling him to step on in and through to the kitchen door. His unsmiling nod and murmur did not bode toward the Walt side of things. Once again, Christian's size impressed me as I followed him into the kitchen. A strong whiff of body odor, way past ripe, gave me that uh-oh kind of feeling, but the thing was already set in motion.

"I don't think you'll find much, Christian, but hey, you can look and maybe there's something in the fridge"; I chatted to his back, following him to the big, almost-empty kitchen. The only furniture was in the living room: a wooden table in the corner with two straight-backed chairs and an old sofa facing the kitchen doorway, sitting low to the floor. Tall sash windows without curtains looked out over the flat roof of the house next door and, in turn, filled the room with bright, gray-white San Francisco light. A worn braided rug, pale in the bright light, provided more sitting space.

Steve and the rest of the guys were at the Dead's house helping with the move to Novato—loading, packing, whatever—I knew there was no one in the attic room or in the apartment next door; they'd all gone together. I was the only one in the group who didn't play or sing; I was the only real old lady—I sewed and cooked and tagged along with Steve. The other guys brought girls home trying to be like Steve and get hooked up with some lost soul who'd take on their well-being as a job of sorts, but mostly they had lots of one-nighters or three-weekers. I suspected that Christian had something on his mind besides garbage.

I had intended to keep the paper bag that held our trash empty, just to thwart him if he did show up, but I'd forgotten. He was on his knees now, going through the bag, and I stood watching him. He came up with two rock-hard doughnuts, turned to me, holding them up in triumph, and asked if I minded if he saved them for later.

"I don't care," I answered, "but I don't see why you'd want to eat them. If you're hungry I can cook some brown rice; I've got a hundred-pound bag." That was the way back then; if someone was hungry, we always shared. I tried to put some distance and authority in my voice, which I knew sounded a bit less than hospitable to let him know I would fix food, but that was all. He was still on his knees with the doughnuts, which he wrapped carefully, and I could feel my brain cornering to his like a boxer preparing for the fight; it didn't take long. Christian was stroking his long beard as if absently, then he looked up and gazed at me as my stomach dropped with disappointment—not fear—disappointment that I never attracted cool guys who could think of a damn thing in my presence except sex, unless of course, they were taken—then they just left me alone. The moustache gesture was doubly repulsive, its similarity to masturbation, as if he were sitting there petting himself and dreaming of pussy while he prepared his pass. I couldn't stand it when Steve petted his own blonde mustache either.

"You know, Merimee, you really are pretty," he said. "Come over here and just let me touch you. That's all I want." He reached out with the offending hand. I had no impulse to run—men were too much like dogs. I hoped that if I were nice, he'd be grateful enough to behave and would leave peacefully. I stood near enough so he could put his hand on my hip. His stench was nauseating. "Christian, I think it's time for you to go now," I enunciated clearly, each word.

Steve and I had a loose relationship—no rules—we knew we were in a time for inventing new ways. We cheated on each other sometimes, but nothing ever came of it, and I'd come back after leaving him once already. I didn't sleep with the other guys in the band, which would've seemed like incest, and I knew Christian was not someone I'd have sex with willingly, even if he was right there and his horniness was filling the room. I weighed the pros and cons quickly, not wanting to be unfairly prejudiced. Stud service, yes, but he stank. If he'd come courting, I thought, he certainly should have bathed first. Reeking was just out of the question if you were trying to roll around with someone you barely knew. The guy was crazy, not just eccentric.

By this time his arm had slipped around my waist and the other one had come up and locked me in, all in a split second. He was pressing my side with his hairy head. "For God's sake, Christian," I told him, "don't you ever take a bath?" But he didn't answer. He was moaning and rocking and holding on as if I were a tree in a hurricane.

"No, this isn't going to happen," I said again, through my teeth. Then, "Get your hands off of me!" and started pushing hard on his arms, but he wasn't letting go.

"Please," he begged. I was surprised at "Please," a large man begging on his knees for my body, but it was more like he was a little kid whining at his mom for a piece of candy. "I need you," he sobbed. "I am a man and I need a woman."

Oh great, I thought, another thing I particularly hated, being glommed into one great mass of women that this guy was in need of, as if my own individual body were just an available outlet, the nearest place to plug in. "Christian, let go of me!" but he only held tighter; I sank my fingers into his nasty hair and pulled hard. He threw his head back, letting up his grip just enough for me to break free.

I didn't want to be known as someone who would have sex with stinky Christian Larson. It would get out and I'd be really embarrassed, as if he were the best I could do. No one would believe I hadn't asked for it, that I couldn't have gotten away if I wanted to.

I ran through John's room, through the bathroom, and into our room. I could lock the bathroom so he had to go back around to the hall door. By that time

I was barricading the door. He was pounding yelling, "Please, Merimée, please!" I found myself laughing at the idiocy of it as I dragged my big leather trunk, heavy with clothes and junk, and wedged it against the door. He was thumping up and down the hall, shouting, "I need you, Merimee; I want you!" Like what he wants is really important to me, I thought, getting ready to push, bracing my feet on the bed. God, what a loser. What a lot of fucking nerve.

"Go away, Christian, leave me alone," I screamed several times. The door bulged as he pushed and I pushed back, thinking how he could actually just crash through the plywood center panel if he really wanted to. "Go away now, Christian; I'm not having anything to do with you!" I made a mental note to be more careful about interesting bums.

Then he stopped. I heard him say, "Hey, man," and knew he had slipped past whoever was entering the front door of the apartment, as if he'd been on his way out the whole time. I went into the kitchen and found Steve reaching around on the top of the fridge, retrieving some dope he had stashed in a tiny pouch. Steve's sea-blue eyes and tall good looks were a real currency for the band. "Hey, you wanna come back over with me?" he asked, not noticing anything unusual. "There's food cuz it's Phil's old lady's birthday, and they're not really moving 'til tomorrow." He was getting the pack of papers from the little basket and stuffing it all in his tight, bluejeans pocket.

"Yeah, I guess." I knew he wouldn't be sympathetic to my inviting some guy up to the apartment and then whining about things not working out very well. "Are you guys still playing the gig in North Beach tonight?" I asked him, thinking through to where the day was going next, very glad I'd lucked out with a rescue. Walking into our room to get a coat, I called out, "Do you know that hairy guy that was walking out of here when you came in? Well, if he ever comes around here again, would you please not let him in?" Steve was standing in the room now, watching me put on my fringed, buckskin jacket and noticing the trunk in an odd position. I pulled my hair up over the collar, and then asked him to help push the furniture back in place.

"Yeah, but what happened? Did you fuck that guy, baby?" He turned me toward him and put his hands on my waist, looking in my eyes and grinning. He was always grinning, as if every damn thing was funny, unless he was angry or asleep, or singing to girls in the audience. I twisted away from his grip.

"I did not! And I didn't want to, but he seemed to think I wanted to. Jesus, he chased me around the whole apartment." Steve stood there, listening, one hand on the doorjamb now, looking entirely too disinterested. I emphasized Christian's aggressive behavior. "I think he might've raped me if you hadn't walked in right then."

"Well, you go around looking like you want it, Baby," he said turning and starting to walk towards the front door.

I was incredulous at this idiotic response, as if I'd been slapped for insubordination. "I look like I want it?" I repeated back, feeling anger that I knew wouldn't surface entirely. I sensed that he wasn't going to understand or care enough. I became aware of my breathing again and thought of words lingering on my vocal cords. "I look like I want it?" was all I could say; I felt disgust towards his hypocrisy. I felt the life-long abandonment that was the norm for me. "How the hell am I supposed to look?" but it came out too flatly, too quietly. He didn't respond, but I heard my own thoughts clearly. I will not live my entire life with this arrogant man. He doesn't even care how I feel.

"Come on. Let's go," he said. Lead singer and bass player for the band now, he was eager to get back to the Dead's, around the top of the hill and down on Frederick Street. Holding the door for me with his arm up, I slipped under; he kissed my neck as I walked by, leaning down to brush my cheek and hair with his lips. He wrapped his arm around my shoulders as we walked to the stairs on the big, carpeted landing which had probably been elegant some fifty years before. It would be a while, I thought to myself, but I will get away from him. I resented his conciliatory touch.

Merimée Moffitt

Carol and the Dead

Outside, the afternoon air had turned wet with fog and the sting on my cheeks felt good. I loved the way the ocean entered the air in San Francisco. When we got to the stoop of the Dead's Victorian flat, a prettier and more expensive one than ours, I was hungry and glad there'd be food.

It was Jerry himself who let us in, in his usual state of excessive black hair, a tee shirt and jeans. He was always just a bit chubby, the kind of guy, who didn't think of himself as good-looking. I suppose he was the designated door guard, or else the ante-room was simply a cool spot to practice his new riffs, which is what he was doing. He could answer the door, say hello and usher us in, without even putting his ax down. "Hey, Merimée, nice to see you." Smile, peck on cheek. "You guys go on in and get some food before it's all gone." He went on with whatever he was plucking out, sitting back down in a mahogany armchair with tapestried upholstery, his head bent down in concentration. The little front parlor was paneled in ornate wood work as were many of the nicer flats in the city. I noticed they hadn't gotten much moving or packing done; the parlor still had chairs and the elegant mirror with hooks around it for hanging coats. We left ours on and walked into the next room where people were eating and talking in the semi-dark. As we entered the living room, I could hear lots of people elsewhere in the apartment. One little Tiffany-like table lamp was on in a corner. Some people were standing with plates; others were seated on a dark sofa. A circle was forming, on the rug, of people passing a joint around, and Pig Pen reached up to offer me the requisite toke. I didn't much want to get high but took a social drag anyway and turned to hand it to Steve, but he had disappeared into the kitchen. I sat down politely to be part of the ritual until the joint was gone.

One of the girls I didn't recognize obviously knew Steve; she had gotten up just as I sat down, and she followed him into the next room, and I felt a wave of anxious jealousy, maybe just territorial angst—he was my everything and I didn't want him getting lost. I was so attached and insecure and needed him even if I knew it wouldn't be forever. This girl had a perfect figure. I noticed the trim waistline that sloped right into her jeans and nice-looking full breasts under a clinging shirt; her mop of dirty blonde hair was not unlike Steve's. They'd look good together. There were people talking in the other rooms and sounds of children shrieking in play. When I went into the kitchen, the girl was standing very close to Steve, and they both turned to look at me as I entered. The table held platters and bowls, remnants of the meal, but neither had a plate in their hands. They continued to look without speaking.

"Hello," I said, expecting an introduction. I moved next to Steve who kindly put his arm around my waist and introduced Carol, who took a very good look, as if assessing her competition.

"Hi, nice to meet you," she said, smiling right into my face, close enough to kiss if I'd leaned just a bit forward, but I didn't want to kiss this wholesome-looking girl, who glowed like an ad for a California health spa. Well, I like her too, I thought, but not enough, not as much as Steve does. I decided to ignore Carol and hope that she'd waft off in another direction.

A homemade poppy seed cake had already been cut and mostly eaten, but there was still salad and bread and some spaghetti left. I'd never been in this room before, so I looked around as I scooped up food. Nothing in the kitchen seemed to have been moved. The walls were decorated with collages in antique frames. Antique cooking utensils hung from hooks on the wall. I could see a stack of cardboard boxes in a pantry closet. The stove was the twenties kind I loved—a light green enamel gas range that said "Mother" on the oven door, and I wondered if Frank Zappa had one like it. I liked Zappa's crazy lyrics. With a filled plate, I went back in the living room. Steve and Carol were fixing plates too, as if that's what they'd been in the kitchen for.

The circle had dispersed and two people were lying on the rug side by side now, talking quietly. Three of the guys in the P. H. Phactor came out of the practice room putting on coats, telling Steve, who was eating cake, that they'd see him over there (at the Matrix), the Jug Band's three-nights-a-week gig. We would be riding the Honda; they'd go in the old Caddy convertible that was the only other vehicle, along with all the instruments. I knew we'd talk about Carol eventually, but when I asked him, he said she was just some girlfriend of Phil's old lady. He'd never seen her before. He was lying.

Carol wasn't mentioned again until the Dead got all moved down to Novato in the valley, and they invited everyone to a housewarming. The new place was a mansion with a pool and porches and pastures and vineyard all around, and of course, Carol was there.

I'd packed us a lunch in a big paper bag that day, and we drove down in the Caddy, alone. Everyone else was coming later with other rides. It was a terrific place out in the middle of nowhere in wine country and must have cost a fortune to rent, but the Dead's success was skyrocketing, what with Owsley's backing and all. I was beyond envious when I saw the three-story colonial house with a driveway about a mile long, but happy that someone got to live there and that the sun was shining for the swim party.

Jerry'd been watching for us, it seemed, at least he said so. He and Steve were buddies, and as soon as we parked, he came rushing across the back lawn to the field where people were lining up cars. Today he was in a black tee shirt and brown jeans. "Hey, Steve and Merimée, here," he said as we met him on the tree-dotted lawn that rolled up to the deck of the pool. "Here, I've been saving this for you, but there's only one left. Sorry, you'll have to split it." He held out a little dot on paper, looking happy about everything, the way he always did. Maybe it was the size of their new pad or the numbers of cars parked for the party—I got the feeling for the first time that the Dead was going to get very big, that having Jerry Garcia save me some acid would be a story for my kids some day. But I was too uptight; I didn't wanna blow my mind—whatever was left of it. I said no thanks, not today. I didn't want to ruin this beautiful day with some whacko acid trip. Picnics, especially picnics near water and on a warm sunny day were special, reminiscent of the only times my mother had spent away from cooking and cleaning, happy times. Jerry looked disappointed, but I didn't care. He wasn't someone I felt I had to impress with psychedelic bravado. Perhaps these were early signs of wanting to survive, to find my own path rather than an eternal run with the lemmings. Maybe he'd been planning something wonderful in his own personal psychedelia, but I wasn't buying it. I'd stick with the beer and sunshine.

It was going to be a great party. People were arriving with food and drinks. The Dead were already set up on the porch that looked out at the pool, with a balcony over them where people could view the whole scene and dance or whatever. I ignored the feelings of inadequacy about vetoing the acid. Steve had gobbled the tab, and I said I'd take care of him, be his guide if he got lost in space—his designated trip master.

We laid our blanket on the grass which was filling with partiers. Girls in bikinis didn't wait too long to take off tops and call it a topless party. Steve had on some cut-offs and was tan as usual. I looked for familiar faces, wandering among the blankets, chatting with a beer in hand, feeling self-conscious about my toplessness, but just going with the flow on that one.

The Dead were trying out their new, extra-sized equipment that Owsley had bought them. Owsley was there with his wife who was very funny because she was so hopelessly straight. I found them arguing in the upstairs hallway in the main part of the house when I went to take a pee. Melissa was out on the roof with her hair in rollers and crying, sitting alone in the bright sun, fully clothed. She never participated in any way except trying to drag Owsley back home. I never saw her do anything else. Owsley had his foot up on the windowsill pleading with her about something.

Once the Dead got things going, girls were dancing on the corner posts of the balcony above the band; Neal Cassidy (Dean Moriarty in Kerouac's novels) was dancing drunk and topless, too, on his blanket with his woman and some kids—maybe his. I stared for a long minute or two, but the Cassidys weren't mingling. Neal held a cigarette high in his hand, dancing in faded jeans, barefoot, his belly still a rippling six-pack. He seemed really drunk. And old, but I knew this also was an historic moment—to be so close to him, having no idea, of course, that he wouldn't live much longer.

I was on the blanket with Steve having some sandwiches when Carol stood up on the diving board in her bikini bottom, and I felt a tidal wave of anxiety. I hadn't spotted her at the party or given her much thought really since the dinner, but now there she was, walking out to the end of the board, looking terrific in baby blue bottoms, her perfect breasts pointed straight ahead as she raised her arms in the air to execute a swan dive.

As she climbed out of the pool and back onto the board, Steve said, "She's nice, Baby. She needs a place to live and I was thinking maybe she could move in with us."

I looked at him before responding, sensing the delicacy of the moment, his altered mood and all—the truth-serum effect of the acid. He seemed peaceful and dreamy as he watched Carol take another dive, sitting with his arms around his knees, the sun reflecting off his tanned face, his smile, his maddeningly blue eyes. "You want to invite her to move in with us? Into our little room, our one bed?" I asked. I felt myself running through a consideration of having another woman share our crazy awkward intimacy and kept coming up with screaming negatives. No, no, no was all I could hear. "No way," was all I could muster. "If she moves in, I'm moving out."

"We could just try it," he pleaded. "If it doesn't work out, she could leave." Everything inside me revolted at this notion, because I knew she'd win; he'd chose her and I'd be on the sidewalk again—suitcase in hand. Really stranded, scared. He was talking as if Carol were an Exercycle or a brand of soap, as if she would be a pawn in his little fantasy. That she'd be inanimate, I sincerely doubted. I hadn't met a human yet who wouldn't make one scene after the other in trying to hold on to some kind of love life. I also felt I couldn't possibly compete. She'd be sexier, more happy and complicit to his demands. She'd show me up. I didn't want her to get her foot in the door, even if it was the opposite of hip to say no to a threesome. I said No. Even if I was a she devil from hell, I didn't want to share Steve with another woman. I couldn't even think about it then, probably because I didn't really think about anything in those days. I just reacted. If I'd been able to think about having Carol in our bed, I might have even liked the idea. But my Catholic upbringing easily bent over to let me live in sin with Steve, but to add a sexual relationship with a woman just blew my fuses. I could only view it as an ouster, a set-up to make me leave, to run screaming down the street, even though I'd vowed to myself already that I wasn't going to stay with Steve forever. My plan was to have leaving be my choice.

"You're nuts, and she's not moving in." I looked around for an alternative to sitting on the lawn watching Carol. "Let's go over to the hill under the trees while the sun goes down"; I wanted to get away from the whole crowd. I slipped on my blouse and grabbed Steve's hand—he was in a zombie state. We walked together away from the party to the grassy oak-covered slope, one field past the house and pool.

The setting sun made everything golden, and the music drifted up to us mixed with voices and the quiet of the grass and leaves. Carol and the problem of Carol seemed far away. A few people were already drifting out to the cars and heading home. Sometimes I could be with Steve and feel like one person with him, away from everyone else. We'd been together for so long and my fortune had been thrown in with his through so many changes; this little storm of wanting Carol would pass. He stretched out beside me on the hillside, up on one elbow watching the scene below, not concerned with her. She was just there. That sorrowful feeling swept over me that I didn't really love him, that I didn't have a passion for him that enveloped my senses and made me feel whole and satisfied. It was more like we had fallen in together, and that I'd fall away from him someday, but just not now. Where would I go if I had to leave him tomorrow? It scared me that he wanted more, that I wasn't enough for him. I was failing again. Man I was a mess.

Steve was so high he didn't want to drive, and I had had so much beer and sun by late afternoon that I wanted to sleep it off in spite of the laws being loose, no DWI or DUI enforcement yet—the roads were so much emptier in the sixties—the idea of rush hour was just coming into the vocabulary. We went back to the pool and swam for a while in the cooling light. The crowd was thinning out at dusk, the Dead packing up instruments and going into their house, saying good-bye, good-bye, thanks for coming. Jerry had told Steve and me we could have the little room with the skinny bed in the pool house and to come on in the kitchen for whatever food was left. Carol had disappeared.

The kitchen floor was crunchy with dirt from so many swimmers coming in and out all afternoon. I scraped the bottom of a cauldron for some beef stew to bring out to Steve and shared the last of the garlic bread with Phil and Bob, whose old ladies were off somewhere private. I wasn't sure they even existed. They never mingled.

Steve and I ate outside in the guest room where I found an old flannel nightgown hanging on a nail. It was soft and warm against my sunburned body; the night air was already damp as we made some kind of peace-offering love in the little bed, a platform with an old cotton mattress on it right next to a dirty-paned window. The lights were on in the empty pool, but everyone else was in the house or gone home. I still felt sad, but we slept in each other's arms, a comfortable embrace that warded off the cold. I woke up at dawn, feeling the chance to start all over.

After cleaning up some party litter from around the pool and the long grass, wet with morning dew, we drove back to the city.

Later on in the week, I went to the little place on Haight to wash our clothes, and when I came home, there they were, sitting very close together on the sofa in the living room. I'd come down the hall after dropping two pillowcases full of laundry in our bedroom, hearing quiet voices. And there was Carol, glued to Steve's side, their knees touching; they were actually holding hands. Rage just shot through my veins and filled me to bursting when I saw them, turned toward each other, as if in mid-something-or-other. I stood still for a split second, feeling like a fool; then they turned to look at me, Carol with no expression, Steve with his grin.

It was blinding rage and betrayal—he was dumping me. I ran to our room, slamming the door, looking for something to throw. Shaking with anger and insult all in one, I grabbed a quart-sized mason jar full of raisins and flung it against the wall. The satisfying smash was just right; it thumped and broke and fell in chunks of glass and gobs of raisins all over the low shelf of books. Everything stopped. My rage listened to the silence in the apartment then, my breathing, noisy with crying, hands wet with hot tears and snot. I was so sure my life was shit, but I couldn't stand it just disappearing, being replaced by someone slimmer and blonde and quiet. I hated her and would never ever be able to move over and let her into our life, someone whose claim to fame was being able to dive.

I opened the door with every intention of violently attacking her, but instead, when I went to the door where he was saying goodbye to her, I socked him as hard as I could. She slipped out the door just like Christian had—as if nothing had happened. "You stupid shit," I cried, pummeling Steve on his face and shoulders until he grabbed my wrists and turned me toward our room. Carol never came back.

I was hunched over feeling miserable, weeping now, and Steve bent over me, trying to give comfort of some sort. He said, "It's okay. She doesn't have to live with us. Don't freak out." Big of him. He put his arms around me, but I only felt the depth of my hopelessness, my dependence on him, my clumsy, inept way of living. I hated being calmed by him. Not too much after that, the band got a gig in Portland, and we all decided to move there.

Hanging with the P. H. Phactor

I was the only permanent fixture old lady (aka steady girlfriend, live-in lover) in the band until Diane came along, and no one, including me, would've thought she'd last as long as she did. The first time we met was at our house way up above Goose Hollow, mine and Steve's. The group had just transplanted to Portland from San Francisco in the winter of '66—a disastrous career move, but, of course, no one knew it at the time.

"Diane," John Browne said as he helped her slip off her coat in the foyer of the fabulous old house. Steve and I had spent days sweeping out all the cobwebs and painting the walls of the living room refrigerator white. The woodwork stayed dark and natural; the windows had no curtains. The green of Diane's dress and green-brown eyes linked her to the jungle of berry bushes, ferns, and redwoods that clung to the hillside out each window. Our turn-of-the-century rental consisted of three stories stair-stepping up the side of the gulley.

"This is Diane," he said again, and I got that in spite of his usual caution and cynicism about women, he found her quite interesting. I did too. She, too, was voluptuous, strong-looking, and without any make-up or jewelry or likely even underwear, she glowed attractively in a velvet dress, a twenties-style gown, full length and bias cut.

"Where's your bathroom?" she whispered to me, as Steve and John went into the living room that was used exclusively for practice. The large bathroom was on the same floor, just behind the stairs to the attic.

"Come on," I said. She smiled when I indicated the door just behind us, and we went in together. I was usually alone with the guys, hanging out, listening, waiting, so it made me happy she wanted to be friendly—friendly enough to pull up her dress and pee while I watched. "Hey, nice house," she said, smiling right at me. Her hair was so thick that hanks of it would bend, hitched up on her shoulder. Mostly dark blonde and straight, it had streaks of light and dark, a natural Norwegian look.

"Yeah, it's okay. How long have you known John?" I asked, leaning against the wall, watching her. John was the folk singing heartthrob of Portland who had gone south to San Francisco for no reason anyone would dare to put forth (hard-hearted Lena). The window behind Diane's head as she stood at the sink was dense with Portland shrubbery. We had no need for curtains anywhere.

"I'm living with him," she answered, now peering at herself in the mirror, washing her hands, then splashing her face. "About a month, but it'll be forever too"; she patted her face with my hand towel, then looked in the mirror again. She was big breasted; square jawed, with a slim waist. "I know he's the one; God, I'm so in love with him." These words made her bend and twist, as if she were one of the guys playing an intense guitar riff. "He makes me come almost every time, and I love everything about him."

That tossed the ball to my court. I certainly didn't feel so confident about my sex life with Steve, or any aspect of my life with Steve for that matter. Steve the gorgeous Thunder God, Steve the Adonis, Steve the madman, Steve my old man, Steve the singer in the band, Steve my roommate and lover. Neither of us knew much about love, didn't even think that much about love—having grown up without ever hearing those words spoken. And sex? It happened. All the time. Wild and energetic and crazy, but orgasms? Hmmmm. Was I missing something? Yes, I'd already started throwing Steve off me in boredom—not really understanding a thing about myself, my body, my life.

"How old are you?" I asked, glancing off from any talk of the mysterious O. I couldn't stand talk about orgasms, since I wasn't quite sure if what I did in bed with the guys who ravaged me had to do with me having orgasms. I had no idea how to pay attention to my own sensations. It was all about pleasing him, being there for him. What I liked sexually was being held and needed, being touched and made aware of my nerve endings, assured of my beauty. I hadn't even known the word "orgasm" til a party my senior year in high school when I loudly announced, "What's that?" to someone in a crowd and got laughed out of the room. Black-habited nuns held the keys to my sexuality with their terrorist stories about hell and fire and the thoughts or feelings that would put me there. The nuns stole my orgasms, stole them from me in catechism class. Who was having mine now? Where did they go? I was having them in elementary school, and the nuns terrified the sensation right out of me. Now, in 1966 Portland, I would fuck any one I damn well cared to, in my own kind of revolution against the insanity of life, but I couldn't put simple words on it, like "come" or "love."

"Fifteen," she answered, surprising me. Oh Jesus, I thought; John was at least twenty-seven. He was way too old for a fifteen-year-old girlfriend. But she didn't really look fifteen. It pissed me off that he'd pick her up like a stray kitten. I wouldn't have trusted any of the guys in the band with a kitten, much less a fifteen-year-old girl. "Don't worry," she said, reading my concern. "He loves me; I know he does, and I'm planning on marrying him."

Well, that's a lot of planning you've been doing, I thought, but kept it to myself. I figured her bubble was going to get burst soon enough. And who was I to predict her future?

"Where are your parents? Why aren't you living at home if you're only fifteen?" I asked. I was twenty at the time, and fifteen meant three more years of jail bait for all of us, especially John, not that I expected her to be around that long.

"My mother is insane," she answered, "and I'm never going back."

"Don't you miss your family? Can't you even visit?" Diane said she came from Portland, so she wasn't far from home. My own mother had disowned me the year before, at nineteen, told me not to drop by or call, ever again. She had my father write and tell me the news: I was no longer their daughter. Funny. I remember re-reading, then laughing. It had been like getting divorce papers from my parents, but divorce wasn't popular in those days. Hardly anyone got divorced, and I had no animosity against them. I didn't grant the divorce. It wasn't happy to get the letter, but I knew my parents didn't understand my life or even their own or their own marriage. I thought they were so misguided that I vowed to stay in closer touch. I wrote them and told them they'd be hearing from me often, after that disownment—all about all my adventures. I couldn't imagine cutting myself off from them; they meant something to me, even if it was just memories.

I wanted to hear the details of Diane's estrangement from her family. We'd left the bathroom and were back in the foyer. The drums, guys' voices talking, and someone making guitar squeals let us talk freely near the open door to the practice room.

"I've been gone six months and I don't miss them," she said. We whispered to each other, letting our eyes roam over the guys and their instruments. "My mother really is insane," she said again. "Scary."

"Brothers and sisters?" I continued.

"I'm the oldest of four," Diane explained. "Two younger sisters and a brother. My parents are divorced, but my father parks his car across the street and spies on my mother to make sure she doesn't have any men in the house. He came in once and hit her, and I'm not going back there." It was starting to be an inquisition so we broke off the conversation. Time for tea

The kitchen of that house was at the bottom of three stories; the third floor attic apartment housed our landlady. She had rented to us when we knocked on the attic door that green and damp Portland day after crossing an amazing little catwalk from the curvy street which wrapped itself up the hill. I talked to her after she opened the glass-paned door, Steve standing hopefully behind me. Her ancient, opera-singer face was framed with gray-blonde hair that streamed to her waist. She must've liked the looks of us and rented it to us cheap. She OK'd the paint. We were asked to bring her the rent, cash, on the first of each month. No papers were signed. Each descending floor attached itself to the side of the ravine, and we could have the entire house except her attic room. Her relatives brought her food, she said. I never did spend any time with her; not much sympathy in me or time for other outcasts. Later, when we turned the house over to Hendricks, rumor had it they had become the best of friends, and I was happy for her that he had taken time to be with her.

Diane and I cut across the practice room to the stairs down to the basement kitchen. We made some chamomile tea on the old gas range, an old freestanding thing with the requisite skinny metal legs and the oven to the left of the cast iron burners. We brought the pot upstairs. I could hear Nick on his mouth harp and Paul on drums. From that night on, Diane attached herself to us all with a tenacity liken to the house itself, clinging up there in the Portland clouds. She would cling to John until death eventually parted them, some five children birthed one per year or so until her mental health caught her on the downside and took her out.

Diane became my friend, and things were easy with us. She didn't compete with me for attention from Steve, and I knew, at least, I'd never mess around with her old man either. I wasn't in love with her; I just liked her smile and her attention. We attached like sisters or friends or both. She and John moved into a little Victorian bungalow a couple of hills south from us.

Later that winter Steve's two teeny-boppers, two girls who apparently did everything together including screwing him, started showing up also, even to a practice at our house from which I promptly eighty-sixed them; I couldn't even go to the gigs without seeing them swooning at his feet while he sang. It was fairly revolting to think that at almost thirty, he was toying with girl children just for fun. They pursued him whenever my back was turned. I came home from work one day—I was a model at the Portland Art Museum art school, and he'd loaned one of the teenagers our shiny green car, which she promptly wrecked, too inexperienced, too stupid to remember to pump the brakes. One had long, ironed black hair; the other was chubbier and giggly and blonde. He wouldn't get rid of them, so I moved out and into Diane and John's extra room. It seemed like I was only there for a few hours, maybe days, before John came up with a reason to disappear indefinitely, and Diane and I were left sharing her little gray and white house. We rolled with the blows in those days, smoked, drank tea, took long walks through the city and the hills. There were no phones for the likes of us vagabonds. People either showed up or they didn't.

Lace curtains drifted over long windows leaving the rooms light-filled. The opposite of my former house, this one sat flat on a ledge-like yard, open to light, high above the city, in weathered paint; yellowish, neglected grass sat bent in the yard. Grey-white Portland sky lit the hill on the best of days, darker shades on stormy ones. At first, Diane and I spent hours and hours reading comic books from the store across the street. She'd wake me with tea and Simon and Garfunkel. We'd get high on her meticulously rolled joints then shoplift maple syrup for pancakes I'd make from scratch, buy a comic book, walk miles down the hills into downtown Portland. Our days were spent picking through junk stores and browsing the old stalls that sold produce and that Jewish bakery that made the best poppy seed rolls.

I worked part-time and life seemed almost unbearably simple, in slow time, the nothing-to-do-with-my-life time that was spent with or without Steve. Diane expected John back any day, but I had my doubts. The more and more we felt alone without men, the more unbearable that part grew. We both felt we were nothing without men. Things had gotten boring. I knew Steve had taken up with someone's sister, and with the lovely musician who would attempt to be a singer in the band.

For me the unbearableness meant getting Steve back, which didn't really worry me. I knew he'd tire of the girls and the other women, and I was sure of my hold over him. There was something about the fire between the two of us that wasn't quite out, and if I was wrong, I figured life would get more exciting as I stepped into changes that would bring new events. But I didn't know what new events I wanted. I just wanted him and the crazy activity of his musical life that gave me a comet to follow. The easy path was all I could see in the fog. I wanted him back in my arms, back in my bed, back in my life as friend, pal, and lover. He was my old man and I hadn't really split up with him. I'd just moved out in a hissy fit. I was waiting, taking a hippie sabbatical. But for Diane, things were a little different. She started blowing fuses when John didn't come home to her.

Steve climbed into bed with me one night, just slipped into the always unlocked bungalow and pledged his fidelity to our togetherness: Fire and air, something about need and combustion. "There's no one who matters as much as you do, Baby," he said, already whirling me away to Steve-land in his Greek-statue-like arms. There was no man in Portland more perfectly gorgeous than Steve Mork. His lion's mane, even if he shaved it off—which he did every once in a while—framed a face like those that helmed Norwegian ships, the original white men of our country. I hadn't found him so gorgeous when I first met him; was it our need that had given him beauty? Steve was still my man and there was no escaping yet. He filled my hunger, that empty space in every cell that called out for his skin to be on mine. It wasn't a thinking kind of thing.

Steve had let our house go to John Hendricks, the band's barefoot mandolin whiz who complained that we'd ruined a divine opportunity with so much white paint. Apparently Hendricks had not only charmed the opera singer landlady, but he'd had the rent and Steve hadn't. With no car and no house and his only income the pittance earned by the Jug Band's gigs, Steve started renting Gregg Stockert's attic. Gregg had been our kitchen boy and guitar apprentice when the band lived in the Haight the previous year, and Gregg now rented a lovely gingerbread Victorian in a neighborhood between the Willamette River and Barbour Blvd. The attic room was entered by a ladder propped up through an unfinished crawl space accessed above the back porch. One then had to walk deftly along planks over joists that held the ceilings of the rooms below. Steve had finished the street end of the attic with plywood flooring and built a bed tucked in under the eaves. A tiny window looked out over the neighborhood, letting in enough light to see. There was a large table, a dresser, and a chair. A nice room for a monk or a Steve Mork at the time. I loved it, of course, and moved my stuff and my body in as soon as he invited me. No one was paying the rent on the gray-light house that John had rented for himself and Diane.

The day I packed my meager belongings to follow Steve to his attic and take up my position again as his old lady, Diane showed her first signs of serious mental instability. "John needs to come now," she stated, loudly, sort of to the clouds over my head as I threw things into Nick's car; Nick was the band's brain, and the only car. Diane and I were standing in the dried-up yard and she continued; "Well, I'm going to stand here naked," she screamed, "until he comes back," simultaneously stripping her dress over her head and tossing it aside. I had no idea where John was or what he was doing.

I grabbed her in alarm as she headed for the gate to the street which certainly had cars whose passengers would see her; I tried to shield her beautiful nakedness by putting myself street side as I wrestled her back towards the house. "John'll be here sometime, Diane, but you'll get arrested if you stand in the street, and you're acting crazy." She'd obviously snapped, with eyes rolling and an uncanny determination to stand naked in the winding, hillside road. "This isn't the way to get John back. You don't need him anyway." I tried reasoning with her, thinking she should have some encouragement to make it on her own, all the while twisting around with her and shoving her towards the front door. I figured he'd dump her for sure if she was really this nuts. In hindsight, she might have fared as well or better if I'd just let her get arrested and locked up that day, but we weren't like that. We protected our own from the authorities. The authorities so often proved themselves ignorant, unkind, inept, and mean. But I couldn't protect her much.

She raised her voice: "He has to come back; he said he would and he has to," twisting and falling all over herself, drooling, snotty tears, fighting me to let her run back into the street naked, which I wouldn't.

"Well, he doesn't really have to, and you'd better get used to the idea of him not coming back." I didn't believe in such displays of weakness even though I admired her devotion to John. I wasn't having any success getting her dress on her or getting her strong body back inside until Steve came out and helped in surprised silence. It was dismaying, but we couldn't do much. She was crying by then and we left her like that, sort of in a heap on the sofa. I didn't know anything about real mental breakdowns, not yet anyway.

"Come down to Gregg's and see me," I said, patting her head. "It'll be okay and we're still friends. You'll be okay." I liked her, but I wasn't her damn baby-sitter. Her craziness, just asking to get arrested or get us all busted didn't sit too well with me. There was no room for true craziness in such a marginal life.

Steve and I drove down the hill in his borrowed car to our new attic room. I loved the sound of rain on the eaves, the entry through the ladder and maze of floor joists. If you missed your step on the boards, your foot would go through the plaster right into the room below.

We shared the little kitchen down below which had an antique gas range and fridge, and the long bathroom had a claw-footed tub. Gregg knew I'd cook pots of beans and brown rice, always make plenty for everyone, and loaves and loaves of home-made bread, cornbread, and cakes and apple pies, so everyone in the house seemed okay with me moving in, everyone meaning Steve and Gregg and Gregg's roommates. I refused to worry about Diane. It was hard enough to look out for myself.

When one of Greg's roommates vacated, Steve and I moved into the beautiful front room that had a bay window where I set up my Singer sewing machine. I started sewing for the head shop down by the river—dresses and shirts. The room was comfortable and I loved making money with my hands and my machine with fabric I'd buy cheap on the remnant tables. Diane eventually showed up, rescued by John, and our friendship settled into back-to-normal at least through the sultry Portland summer, 1967.

*Southern Comfort with Janice
and Injustice for All*

The band had steady jobs, but the money was minuscule. John had returned from wherever and moved back in with Diane into a house around the corner from us. I spent my days making clothes for women mostly, simple blouses, dresses, skirts.

When The Dead came to town and the P. H. Phactor opened for them, Diane and I made marshmallow pies and invited them to come over on the Sunday following the gig. We'd been to their parties in the Bay Area, and it seemed appropriate to invite them to our neighborhood. Phil Lesch and Bob Weir showed up, and Diane and I borrowed someone's car to go to the Holiday Inn and try to talk Pig Pen into coming over. He was in his room smoking and playing his guitar, hardly even turned to look at us from his hunched-over position on the side of the bed, a smoke burning in the ash tray, a quart of booze right next to it. "Nah," he said, "I'm not in the mood." He was a guy seriously in need of a good old lady, but I couldn't take the job. Still sore about our failed date in the Haight, he wasn't about to mess with me again, and I had my hands full already. With regret, we left him in that room, and I never spoke to him or saw him again.

That gig was just a stop for the Dead on a tour they were doing in Seattle and Vancouver, B.C., and they invited the Jug Band to come along and open the show for them and for Big Brother, Janis Joplin's band. Seattle was the only gig where I ever go-go danced on stage.

We'd been in our little dressing room and wandering around the maze behind the stage. Everyone's stuff was piled around on the floor and we were just hanging out, waiting. Stage curtains, lots of them, hallways and dressing rooms, people were coming and going, getting dressed, smoking joints, tuning guitars, being nervous—the crowd was certainly the biggest the Jug Band had ever played—thousands seated in a huge auditorium. Nick had dated Janis for a while before she soared to popularity, and she wasn't one to forget her old friends. Phil Hammond, our band's manager, came in and said, "Hey guys. Janis wants to meet all of you, and she says to come to her dressing room."

We filed out liked we'd been invited to see the queen. She was, after all, the queen. The band had opened for the Airplane one night at Bill Graham's place in the City, and snotty Grace Slick had sent word that she didn't like us—we were "too funky" for her image. I always thought poorly of Grace after that—some kind of straight bitch just in it for the money. So much for what I thought, as if it mattered, but the jug band had soul and talent, and Janis appreciated it. In her room, bigger than ours and with a sofa, Janis sat cross-legged on her couch with one of her guys, and her band members made room for all of us to make the traditional circle. I happened to land in the open doorway exactly across from her, standing in my forest-green velvet afternoon dress as she checked me out. There weren't any formal introductions, just smiles and eye contact. The joints went around, and her famous bottle of Southern Comfort. By the time the dope was gone and the bottle empty, it was show time and I was drunk enough to walk out to the go-go spot on stage during the set. Unprecedented behavior for me, and nothing I'd ever repeat.

We were giggling-high backstage when I got the idea to do it. Why not dance to an audience? Diane and I were both dressed to kill in our slinky and form-fitting velvets. Both of us big breasted and braless, I was sure we could pull it off as part of the act. "I'll go if you will," and she nodded in agreement. I danced my heart out to Janis's "Women Is Losers," far enough left that I'm not even sure she knew I was there, or cared. I was glad when the song was over—ten thousand awestruck faces turned towards Janis, with a few up close watching me, just made me know I liked dancing but didn't like being on stage; Diane followed up and went out and danced the next song. Our little claim to fame. We laughed.

When our dancing was done, we went looking for the guys who at first didn't seem to be anywhere backstage. The dressing room was empty. Hendricks, our mandolin virtuoso, came running down the hall towards us adjusting his monocle, long dark hair flying out under his beaver-skin top hat, saying he needed Steve since the cops were about to arrest Paul, our half-Iroquois, half-something else, very long-haired drummer—for loitering backstage. Steve came out from behind a floor-to-ceiling white curtain where he'd been listening to Big Brother, and we all ran out to the loading zone just as two cops shoved Paul up against the cop car, in handcuffs. His face was bleeding and his hair, normally in a tidy pony tail half-way down his back, was mussed up from the scuffle.

Hendricks acted like a master of ceremonies for the event: "Officers, officers, this is Steve Mork, our singer, and he can assure you that we're here legally as performers." Hendricks was wearing an antique gambler's vest, a dress shirt from the Victorian period, and baggy black jeans under which his feet were noticeably bare. My theory was he couldn't afford fabulous shoes, hence deeming all footgear completely unnecessary, much the same way Diane and I felt about underwear. Expensive and unnecessary—a fabrication of marketing directed at straights who knew nothing of the pleasures of free, bare skin on natural fabric, bare soles on mother Earth.

"Your name, sir, and I'll need your driver's license," one cop questioned Steve. The other stood huffing, out of breath after the tussle with Paul, who apparently had resisted arrest.

Steve chose not to address the threatening tone with humility and caution, but spoke his mind: "What the hell are you doing beating up our drummer, man? We opened the show. We have a dressing room backstage."

Diane and I scooted away from the door, keeping our backs to the building, just watching. Steve's golden mane was flowing out over his shoulders, spilling down his back, and his tight pants never carried a wallet. I doubted he had valid ID or a contract for the performance. All three guys had very long hair, an indication in 1967 that they didn't support the US presence in Nam, or marriage, God, or country in the proscribed method of our parents. We were all deviants in the eyes of the law, and the questioning officer shoved Steve, who shoved him back, and then they were both on him and had him face-down, ripping his arms into handcuffs behind his back before they asked him any more questions. One of them kicked him hard in the ribs a couple of times, then held him down with his cop boot while another got Paul into the back of the patrol car. They drove off with Steve and Paul, followed by another car with two more cops.

We all appeared in the courtroom the next morning where the judge upheld the statements of his four officers, all of whom claimed not to have used any force against either defendant or even to have made any physical contact. Paul and Steve were fined fifty dollars each for disturbing the peace, with one year's probation. Without a lawyer, Paul's Polaroid photos of his abrasions were ignored. I was horrified that the original charge was for loitering backstage at their own concert. The band's wages for the night covered the fines, and we left for Canada with two more shows to open.

Merimée Moffitt

Diane

Diane almost got me arrested later that summer in Portland, or rather, we came close to disaster together, but with a reasonable cop. An artist friend in need had sold me an old Karman Ghia convertible for twenty-five bucks. It was beat-up and lacking a starter motor, rusted-out tomato soup colored, but it ran with a push start or a roll down a hill. Not even a problem as there were always hills to park on.

We were on our way to the Clackamas River one warm sunny afternoon, a river that flows into the Willamette just south of Portland proper, near the town of Clackamas. We both liked to swim in the Willamette which was a walk down to some old docks south of our neighborhood, but with the new Karman Ghia, we could explore places outside of town. This particular afternoon, we were both in homemade bikinis; mine was lime green piqué that clung to and emphasized my full figure. Hers was a copy of how I made mine, but generally Diane didn't do much with finish work and buttons and zippers, and she was always just barely contained by whatever she found to wear, ditto on her bikini.

I hadn't registered the car yet, figuring it wouldn't pass inspection without a starter motor and with a bad leak in the brake lines, and my driver's license was expired by a year or two. Diane had a nickel bag of weed in her pocket that she handed me in terror when the siren started screaming behind us. We were already in the town of Clackamas, and I turned into a parking spot under an old tree above the access trail down to the green and lazy river, almost where we'd been headed anyway. The siren brought a shocking vision to me of fifteen years behind bars as I added up all my oversights, stuffed the maryjane under my seat, and hoped to God I could sweet talk the officer into not searching the open, top-down convertible. Possession of pot with an under-age minor in the car was a serious offense in the eyes of many. I knew people doing time in the big house right then for as little as a roach, the leftover butt of a joint, but I'd just gotten careless. Marijuana was still a very serious crime in Oregon, especially the kind that made you feel like staying a little longer at the river on a nice day—really relaxing and satisfying. This was all just a couple years before pot became decriminalized in Oregon: same state, same government, new laws. But on this day, it could still mean five years in a penitentiary.

"God, " I whispered to Diane, trying to control my breathing in the few seconds I had to get my act together; "I hope we get lucky." As soon as he parked under the huge willow in the cul-de-sac, I climbed up onto the back of the driver's seat, old license in hand. The doors didn't work either, so I had to slip over the side of the car, just a peasant blouse over my swimsuit, which made me look sexy, I hoped.

"I'm sorry, Officer, was I speeding or something?" I smiled—standing respectfully about halfway between his car and mine, bare foot and bare legged.

He stood by his car, observing the catch he'd just landed. He looked around me at Diane, and I followed his gaze, all in a slow-mo instant of hoping. She was smiling her best blissed-out and blonde, dazzle smile, just as relaxed as any happy, compliant female could be. "Heck no," he answered in Oregon country-ese. "But I think your turn signals might not be working right, Ma'am." He stayed, miraculously, right by the back of his vehicle, smiling.

I didn't move. "Really? I didn't know," I answered. "Geez, I just bought this car from a guy who said it needed work, and he wasn't kidding," smiling my own sweetest girl smile. Our convertible was half outside the shade of the huge weeping willow. Diane's hair glistened in the sun, giving us only a profile now as she appeared to be watching some small boats on the river, waiting patiently.

"Well, I need to see your license and check your registration, Ma'am. I'll be happy to give you a little time to get those lights fixed." He seemed relaxed, nice.

I approached him with my license as he laid his clipboard on the top of the trunk of his black and white cop car. "You know," I said with an apologetic tone, as if it were the only thing in the world bothering me, "I haven't had time to register it yet either. It's still got the plates from the other owner and I just haven't done the paper work yet." At this point I leaned on the back of his car, watching him fill in his form, giving him a full-cleavage view. It was the only weapon I had, and I wanted the sight of my tanned breasts to disarm him enough so all he'd want was to get away from us.

"You know you need a new driver's license too? This one's expired." He glanced at me, still smiling nicely. He was young and didn't seem too uptight or angry about the fact that we were breaking at least three laws that he knew about.

"I do? Oh my God. I hope you only give me a warning," I cooed. "I don't think I can afford to do all this at once. I'm sorry about the license; really, I just didn't notice. Oh my God," I acted overcome. I hoped that he'd confuse the terror I felt about the weed under the seat with remorse for the expired license and lack of registration papers.

"You girls come out here to swim very often?" he asked, handing me back my license. The entire little parking area we'd stopped in looked out over the wide and deep Clackamas River, just a scramble down the embankment.

"Yeah," I said, standing with him, waiting, as if our conversation were something I was really enjoying. "I love this spot," I went on, gazing out over the river, taking in the beauty of the place I really did love. "We like to swim out here; it's so quiet and pretty. Clackamas is a great little town." I said it in all earnestness, knowing I'd so much rather live in Clackamas than the State Penitentiary. There were houses all around us at the end of the quiet little street.

"Yeah," he answered, surprising me. "I grew up here and it is a great place. You all get that car fixed and the paperwork done, okay? And have a nice swim." He got in his car and drove off, leaving me almost in tears from the strain. It wasn't at all funny, knowing how bad it could've been. I'm sure he had two sets of handcuffs that would've fit us just fine. A simple search and I would have been done for. Some angel somewhere saved my butt that day, and I vowed to be less stupid about drugs in the car. The rest of it didn't worry me much. We drove home as soon as he was out of sight, after dumping the weed down the side of the hill.

Things were going just great for me that summer. Our room downstairs was very cool: a pot-bellied wood stove for heat at night, an old Oriental rug that filled most of the floor, an iron bed the previous tenant had left, an oak table for my sewing machine, a standing lamp with beaded fringe on an old silk shade. Steve had a record player and records and I had a huge steamer trunk for my clothes and things. Diane lived across the street with John and came over to hang out, help me clean up, make tea. My dresses were getting popular enough that I was busy, and any extra inventory went to a little head shop down the street. Then Steve announced we had to move. I liked the money I was making from selling my creations, but Steve wasn't making enough in the band, and he decided to get a job on a dairy farm in Scappoose, a town about twenty miles outside of Portland, west of St. Helens. He was going back to what he knew—the skills of his childhood. Portland wasn't quite enough of a music town to get by on gigs alone. As usual, I simply followed his lead, tagged along to see what was next.

We could see Mt. St. Helens from the Airstream trailer the farmer and his wife rented us. Steve milked cows morning and night, leaving me to commute to my modeling jobs in the '49 Chrysler I'd traded the Karman Ghia for with my Irish-poet friend. It was weird and lonesome being twenty miles outside of town, but I loved the adorable wood-lined trailer home with the tiny kitchen, living room, and bedroom. Back in town, people had been mentioning that they thought something was wrong with Diane, but it was only during her first visit to our trailer that I knew she was really going wacko.

I went and picked her up one day after work to bring her out to the dairy farm, show her what we were up to—a visit. It was raining when we pulled up in the grass under the dripping willow tree where the silver trailer sat. I made a dash for the front door, but Diane said she just wanted to stay outside for a while.

"In the rain?" I asked, puzzled. It was a typically gray and drizzly Portland afternoon. She was in a dress, some cotton, fifties affair, which I knew would get soaked instantly.

"I know what I'm doing," she snapped. "You don't have to bother yourself about me." I didn't understand the anger. Her face was white in the light from the trailer window and already glistening with rain. There wasn't any place to hang out outside on a day like this, and I didn't think she'd go into the farmer's house where his wife probably would've been glad to fix her coffee and dinner. They were like that—really nice, plain, extremely clean people.

"Uh well, okay, Diane," I said, annoyed, one foot on the bottom step that led up to the tiny living room, a bag of groceries in my arm, headed for the miniature kitchen. "Come on in whenever you're ready." I wasn't feeling much sympathy for someone too stupid to get in out of the rain. The trailer was warm and bright inside. I put on water for rice, wondering what to do. My good friend was standing outside, and I was getting the helpless feeling that this was way more than I could handle. I couldn't drag her into the trailer for the dinner I'd invited her to. She'd seemed okay when I picked her up at her house, but she'd made me promise to bring her right back home after dinner, as if she had too much to do. John was gone again; that was it. John had dumped her and she wasn't making it. By the time the water boiled and the brown rice was poured in and settled to a simmer, Diane had been outside long enough. I went out and found her on her knees in the rain, apparently praying aloud, talking to someone in the now dark, dripping sky, her face uplifted. Rain and tears were mixing on her face.

"Diane," I squatted down beside her. I felt very frightened that she was so unreasonable. No one sane wanted to be out in the rain with no raincoat, doing nothing. It was scary to see her so disconnected to her body. She seemed oblivious to my presence, or annoyed by it, shrugging me off, continuing a tearful and rambling conversation with some invisible entity. "Diane, you'll get pneumonia out here." Her arm was very stiff at her side, as if she were frozen into place. "Please come inside with me now. This is crazy." She was kneeling in mud, stiff and soaked.

"I'm not coming in your house," she turned at me in anger. "I want everyone to just leave me alone," and she started babbling again as if saying a rosary, but I didn't think she was Catholic. Okay, I thought, getting up. I'm pissed now. She's not coming in, but I'm certainly not leaving her out here praying in the rain.

I went to the barn and got Steve to help me force her into my car. I took her home. By the time we got back to her house, the trance seemed to have passed. She went into the house, and I didn't see her again until she showed up at another Portland pad of mine, almost two years later and six months pregnant.

For Steve and me, the farm was pretty much the end. We tried moving back to town, another attic; he had quit the band or they kicked him out—it was dreary. There were too many drugs, winter had arrived in Portland and my heart, and his teeny bopper was pregnant, by him. I told him I'd be taking the car and heading south one night after work. The plan was to go to Eugene, meet up with my sister, and move back to San Francisco. Not a deep plan but what is referred to now as the geographical cure. Maybe just doing something was better than nothing. I couldn't let him be my leader any more. He had even asked me if we could adopt the teeny bopper's baby. It just made me heartsick. I had to go—somewhere, anywhere, and in my need for hope, I'd devised a plan that all I had to do was wait until Randy got out of the Army. Then we'd get married and all would be OK. Randy had been a brief affair the summer I was home after New York and before running off to the Red Dog. Randy would save me. That was the plan; I just had to wait a year for him to come back. The thing with my sister fell flat, and I found myself homeless about a week after arriving in San Francisco.

Merimée Moffitt

Fell Street on the Panhandle

It was like bread and butter right from the start with us: Mushy needed an old lady and I needed a pad. Mushy, whose given name is Marshall, had been on Haight Street that night as I waited for the light to change; he was on the corner waiting to cross, and me in my car, right there, first in line, planning to cruise the entire Haight before I went to my date with the pimp I'd met the day before in North Beach. The pimp also ran a topless joint, but he'd said, "You'd do better dishing it out on your back," and I was desperate enough to make a date with him, hoping something would come up in the meantime. The cruise down Haight was some last ditch chance to find whatever it was that would save my butt from turning a real trick, and there he was—my Godsend. His face just lit up when I tapped on the horn, and mine must've too, and he was jumping into the car next to me, flesh 'n blood: life was good and I'd been rescued again.

God was I happy to see Mushy. He was cute enough, a boyish kind of cute—skinny, tall, an easy-going freak on the scene, bad skin and pretty eyes in a not-too-handsome face—thinnish, non-descript brown hair that wouldn't grow long. Not the kind of guy who could make women swoon for him for no reason at all, but he did have a manly lankiness about him, and legs that were made for bell bottoms. He slid across the seat of my old Chrysler and kissed me as if we'd planned the whole thing—some kind of cosmic date, his brown hair falling across his eyes, a bit nervous as always, too, from living on the edge for so long.

"Hey Baby," he said, eager. "You're the only person in the whole world I want to see right now." He kissed me on the lips as he closed the door, and it felt good. A warm body wanting me, a friend, not some goddamn North Beach, fat-assed Italian pimp. We could make it, me 'n Marshall, no doubt in my mind. My stress level had melted down a bit, close to normal, back to business as usual. He was playing his cards for me, kissing me, jumping into the car like it was all meant to be, and I was glad, too. It was so cool to have the old Chrysler to pick him up in—two-tone baby blue, 1949, cherry—the dash board all celluloid and perfect, gray wool upholstery as pearly as our young souls in search of life on the planet. The necessities: a guy, a car, a pad.

Mushy is exactly my age and a sweetie, really. We'd made it once before—nicely tucked away in my memory—in my front-room pad in Portland when my Steve had gone off to open for the Doors, and I was tired of back-stage rooms and traveling all night in vans and all that stress of trying to hang with the stars. Mushy's lean, light body just comfortable, not heavy and pushy. I liked him then, so it wasn't at all sad to see him now. I needed a pad and had about a buck left to my name. The gas in the tank and some clothes and stuff in the car was all. No job, no dough, no place to go, and to tell the truth, I'd been a little worried about the pimp in North Beach. Not someone I'd really want for an employer. So all this flashes through my mind as Mushy slides over the seat to give me a kiss and close the door. I'd much rather give it away or at least trade straight across with a friend. And here's Mushy, dropped from heaven, sitting shotgun now and telling me how to get to his apartment on the Panhandle.

We go to his pad which he says has just been vacated by lousy roommates he kicked out, and he's sick still with hepatitis like he'd been in Portland months before, and could I move in and take care of him, if I wanted to? "You live here alone?" I ask him, knowing this totally cool apartment would be a little out of his single-freak price range.

"I had roommates," he says. He's on his back on the bed, a mattress and box springs, and I'm talking, sitting next to him, getting the situation clarified.

"And they're gone?" I query. The place is almost empty, but beautiful empty: hardwood floors, tall sash windows, one window is placed diagonally in the corner past the fireplace. I know there must be a woman not too far away, but I also know I'm taking the job the second we set foot in the Victorian house. He has the whole second-story flat, and it looks like a refuge I can't possibly say no to, even though a little guilt sets in about using him like that. "No old lady?" I pressure him to be straight with me right away.

"Nah," he says. "I kicked her out. She was a real bitch." I feel I might never love him like a lover should, but hey. This is opportunity knocking. No fire, no brimstone. He's got his arms behind his head, kind of staring at the ceiling while I process the information from our discussion. A kind of weariness seeps into my soul that I'm saying "I do" to Mushy just like that, but I have not one night anywhere to fall back on. I'll give it a try, I think to myself, as long as I'm honest about leaving in nine months when R musters out of the Army—my not-so-secret mad plan for future happiness.

Mushy gets me down next to him, trying to get a little pussy at least before I bolt or the fantasy bursts. It's ok, but not really hot. Feels a bit like work, and I'm sad. But, like I said, in my mind I'm still in the beginning of giving it a try. It isn't as friendly and fun as it was in my pad in Portland, more like "let's see the goods." It's his house now, and I'm screwing him for a share of it. At my house in Portland, I'd had lace and brocade curtains up and an old Oriental rug and beaded lamps and coals smoldering in the wood stove, and it was my scene.

"Mushy," I tell him, "I'll live with you, but I'm not staying forever because I'm waiting for this guy to get back from the Army."

"Well, when's he getting back?" he asks me.

"I don't know, a year or so," I tell him. I'm completely sure that R is the guy for me. His face is an old friend, a light at the end of the tunnel for me to use in the dark. "He's getting out next November, and I'm going to go live with him when he gets back; I think it's only fair that you know this, that we've been writing and he wants to marry me and I'm going to."

"Yeah, well okay. Maybe he'll get killed first, and I can have you all to myself." He nuzzles into my arms and neck and sticks his dick in me and comes again after a few pumps. I don't care. He feels nice and warm and I like being held by him. I like him enough. He's a friend, my own age—his skin is soft and pleasant. For the first time, I really do feel like a whore. It's a contract, a verbal contract between us, but I am desperate enough to do worse, like turn real tricks. Marshall seems like a Godsend. I am grateful and relieved to be taken in and I'm curious about what a relationship might be like with him. After all, he was the one who seduced me first in Portland, and I was pleased.

We're sleeping when his ex-girlfriend's new old man comes in, snaps on the ceiling light above us and starts pulling the blankets and top sheet off the bed. The guy is tall and not at all introducing himself; he's just grabbing the covers and we're lying there looking at him, squinting, and he says, "Hey, these are her sheets and blankets, man, and I'm takin' 'em." I gather that this guy was sent to fetch the bedding, or these two people would be spending a cold night somewhere. Mushy handles it just right.

"Hey, man, it's cool," he says. "Just leave us the bottom sheet 'cause it's mine anyway."

"That's cool," the guy responds quite reasonably, I'm thinking, since we're both of us butt-naked on the mattress that bears the bottom sheet, and the guy knows he'd have to fight us for it. Sleepy as we are, we win this one. The tall guy leaves with his arms full, all in a huff, and I hop up and get my almost-scratchy Indian blanket to put over us. It has a man and a woman on it in bright blues and yellow and white wool. The man has a little hat and the woman's hair is in braids, and they are forever side by side, looking out together, bound in warp and weft. So far, my life is just like that, always bound to a man, warp and weft. It's all I know at the time.

Mushy shows me around in the morning light. "I do still have one roommate left," he says, "but she works all day so we won't see her much." He's tall enough to make me feel good standing next to him, willowy, easy in his body. Shirtless and barefoot this morning, he's a bit skinny with hardly any hair on his chest, just a few strays between scrawny nipples and undeveloped shoulders, but I like how he's tan.

I've been taken in off the streets and have to earn my keep, so I pay attention during the tour of the new scene. His roommate's room is in the back, a little cubbyhole with a double mattress on the floor and clothes all over, but sun streams though a manila-colored shade, making the mess look warm. I ask him who she is, besides a remaining roommate. "She's pretty strange," he says. "I don't really like her, but she pays on time." He stands at the door while I step in and look around a bit. He yawns and stretches, scratches his head. I get the picture. They aren't attached. Her room is seriously not charming.

"What's her name," I ask, still wondering if she'll present a problem—a woman not for him, apparently, but living with him any way.

"Helen, I guess," he says, "but we call her the White Witch." I like that right away, a woman called the White Witch living in a tiny, sunny room with no furniture: clothes and a mattress, beads, incense, dishes, garbage, a few books on the hardwood floor. A temporary-looking existence, no shelves. "She's into weirdo voodoo or something," he mumbles. I assume that she's not a threat, probably just not his style.

We discuss his "business" the next morning when I ask him how he's making money. He has a connection that he distributes for. "You can be my assistant," he says, "to help me keep track of stuff and remind me of things."

"Okay," I say, and I feel good to be wanted. I'm feeling more and more secure. "I'm your assistant. Let's go shopping and get some things to make bread with." I always make bread wherever I'm living, to spread it with tahini or honey and peanut butter or almond butter—fresh, warm, soft, half whole wheat, half unbleached white. You can darn near live on bread like that, and fruit and cheese. We buy groceries and royal blue paint for the dreary, dirty-white cupboards.

I slip into an easy routine with Mushy: walks in the neighborhood, shopping for grocery items so I can make meals for us, friends of his come by, we see movies downtown. For fun, I sunbathe across the street in Panhandle part of Golden Gate Park or catch the bus out to the Marina and swim with the old guys who do laps in the bay like walruses and seals. Mushy comes along and lies next to me in the sun, and I like that, being with him at the beach. We paint the whole kitchen; he buys me a turtle for a house pet.

One night he introduces me to his connection, a white-woman-in-a-fancy-apartment kind of person, but I never see them really doing anything like dealing. That all happens more or less behind my back. Mushy leaves for a while, does something, and then comes home with a little money and weed to smoke. We don't have a phone, and no one ever comes to visit except a few of his friends and his sister. The rent covers utilities too. The Haight is crazy with people, so it's an easy living just selling a little pot now and then, apparently.

Mushy buys me a new, used, Singer portable that I make clothes and do mending on—my own or for friends or trades, sometimes for drugs or money. I make him some blue velveteen bell bottoms; he has me take the bells down a bit. He's too shy for really big bells. He looks long and lean in them, especially shirtless.

Time passes, weeks, then months.

I'm truckin' down Haight Street one morning, early, maybe ten or so, getting some juice and raisin bran muffins from the old bakery on Haight to bring back to the apartment. Pretty morning, energetic—weaving through the crowd, the San Francisco air fresh and sparkly like only salt air in that city of white buildings can be. Haight Street is so full, people are spilling off the sidewalk, cars can barely move; I'm dance-walking along, in and out of multi-colored freaks in tie-died or tattered imports, or hand-made silks and velvets, Goodwill stuff from bins in the storefront on Haight, someone's goodwill. This morning I am in wide-legged damask pants, curtain fabric, made for a dance in Portland, one I'd actually bought some alligator dancing shoes for—forest green. I only wear selected junk, handmade dresses and skirts from salvaged scraps, tablecloths, curtains, bedspreads. My art is what goes on my body—the look and feel of it, the experience of cloth to skin, the freedom of movement and comfort rating higher than the price tag which is gauged in hours of searching or sewing. I don't use money for much other than food, and maybe shoes, bus fare—natural fibers feel good to move in.

Walking with a dollar snatched from Marshall's pants' pocket, the neighborhood looks like a foreign bazaar as usual, because every day is like that in the ghetto of the Haight, desperado kids from just about everywhere. I'm halfway back home when I spot that short freak, Harold from Portland, wending his way through bodies on the sidewalk between us. "Hey Baby," Harold waves to me and opens his arms for a big hug, one which put my breasts about under his chin.

"Hi, Harold," I hug back. He's so smiley and happy to see me even though I hardly know the guy. I'm flattered enough to chat a bit, also figuring that I haven't seen him around the scene in ages. "Where've you been?" I ask, sensing that he does want me to care, must be lonely to be so ecstatic to see me whom he hardly knows. Harold, short as a dwarf as far as I was concerned, and way too hairy. Dark hair flowing from him everywhere.

"Oh, Baby," he dramatizes, a shred of a New Jersey accent, a Jewish boy gone wild. "I been outta the country; Afghanistan, just got back," he says, reaching up to a pendant hanging around his neck, which looks like a half-pound chocolate bar on a rope; he breaks off a corner and puts it in my hand. "Just for you, Baby, and watch out. This is really good shit, really good stuff." He's enthusiastic, sincere; I'm flattered and grateful to receive such a gift.

"Hey, thanks, Harold." I close my palm over the chunk, and know I'll be a hit when I bring this home for breakfast. I'm wondering why in hell I would be so special to Harold who's carried the dope-on-a-rope across oceans and rivers back to the Haight, and now the contents are much more obvious to the casual on-looker, or the not-so-casual cops. But it's a sunny morning and I feel fine, smiling down on his face that just trekked the Himalayas or something; I doubt if he'd shaved or cut his hair the entire trip. He's kinda cute, but way too short for serious loving from me. It'd be Snow White getting it on with one of the dwarves. He hugs me again, but Harold just doesn't do it for me, no three cherries in the slot machine. We do not make a date. I head on home with the dope in my fist.

Mushy pulls out his pipe when I show him the gift from Harold, and we smoke ourselves into another dream-state, an extended morning siesta, a wipe-out which turns off the clock until we get up all over again in the afternoon. Mushy's friend had left his magic markers, and we spend the rest of the day drawing detailed paisley patterns on my tan legs. I skip the bathing routine for a while so I could show them off on the street, and to my parents who were dropping by to take me to lunch.

My parents never mentioned my disownment after Steve and I split up. Perhaps they were just disowning him; perhaps they accepted my counter-offer to stay in closer contact. I didn't accept that they could disown me, and so, on this day the plan was to drop by my pad and meet Mushy. Later, after leaving him too, and showing up in Oregon to wait for Randy to get mustered out and find me and be my next rescue prince, my mother admitted to liking Mushy. That surprised me mostly because she never liked anything that I had to say, anything I did. And it didn't matter anyway as he and I would split up. What I didn't know at the time was that I was looking for independence, and that I wouldn't be finding that inside any handsomely packaged lover. I was headed for the desert, eventually, both literally and figuratively, where I would have to rely on, and consequently get to know my own strengths.

The afternoon my parents show up, I am living art. I am loved. Mushy's art on my legs was the kind of attention I felt starved for. Fun, affection, easy-going stuff. I suppose that's why I hid in pot smoking; the pot high forced an illusion that all those things were happening, or maybe he really did love me. There was a be-in in the Panhandle that day and I suggested to my parents we meander through the park on the way to Haight Street. My mother in her heels, Channel-type suit, and little handbag stood in the middle of the park full of hippies while a band played at the far end. "They don't look like they're having fun," she stated.

"They're just not drunk, Mother," I coldly replied, taking a dig at her alcoholism. "They're stoned mostly on marijuana and that makes people kind of relax, get quiet, not loud and obnoxious." I added that they were having a perfectly lovely day, as far as I knew, and to not worry about them.

When we got up to Haight Street, my dad wanted to get ice cream in the old soda shop that was doing a brisk business. My mother refused, saying she'd lost her appetite. All these dirty-looking people sitting around, wandering around. "It makes me feel sick," she said, summing up the beginning and end of her adventure. I didn't see dirty people, but colorful ones: long hair, long beards, outlandish outfits, dancing and laughing. Haight Street that year was a mecca for young people who wanted to change the world and it's unpleasant rules, and I was part of it.

Free Love, Free Fall

Towards the end of the summer, Mushy tells me we have to go to Arizona for a working vacation. I don't really believe him when he tells me the pot he sells is purchased from the Phoenix Mafia. How could a large group of dark-haired, dark-suited thugs survive in a sea of sun-loving Arizonans? I can't tell if he's kidding or what. His stories about meeting them at mountain caves outside of town pique my imagination, but it isn't of any more real concern to me than how my dad brought home such huge amounts of dough—he sat at a desk and bought and sold lumber. "Buy cheap and sell dear," my father once told me in response to my teenage inquiry. Mushy's pot and the connections don't much matter to me. I seriously don't think pot or smoking it is evil, and he keeps most of his dealings way out of my sight anyway. The war in Nam is evil—the sending of my friends and family to kill strangers who aren't harming us, who aren't a threat to us—The War, is evil.

Simple. We're going on vacation to visit his buddies in Phoenix: golden boy J.D. and J.D. and Barry's pretty girlfriends Darrell and Liz. Barry is on his way up—two to five in Arizona's big house, probably the real reason for our visit. Barry is giving Mushy and me his tomato-red, vintage Ford pickup to keep while he does his time, and we are on our way to drive it back home to San Francisco. We fly to Phoenix, stand-by, cheap, and catch a cab to the address.

In Phoenix, J.D. and Barry have a traditional hacienda with cool tile floors and thick adobe walls. Outside in the blaring, white-walled desert gardens, giant yuccas sit in corners guarding neatly planted strawberry beds. Inside, some of the rooms have no furniture, but the adobe catches and holds coolness from the night.

Within minutes of looking around, marveling at the lacquered floors and adobe walls, we smoke some dope then go to eat in a neighborhood Mexican restaurant. I'm pleasantly aware of having fun eating chips and drinking beer, waiting for tacos. Daryl and LZ are thin, tan, and beautiful, and their easy claim to that desired state of being is a wonder to me. I'm always a bit self-conscious of my extra-large-size body.

After getting back to the house, everyone walks down to the irrigation ditch because it is a freaky hot Phoenix afternoon, and the cold ditch water is inviting, even though it looks awfully fast to me. Initiation time. Maybe they think I'm taking Mushy for a ride, so they're gonna give me one, too. We all get naked, leaving skimpy summer clothing in a pile by the bank. They all double-dare each other to jump in and not get washed away, but it must be an act. Having grown up in Phoenix, they're teasing me, the northern California/Oregon girl. I've never even seen an irrigation ditch. Standing in the shade just inches from the concrete edge, I'm nervous about the current but refuse to be the only hot one, a hot chicken. I figure these people have been cooling off here under drooping elms and cottonwoods, forever; they won't let me drown, probably. The water is freezing and rushing so fast it takes all my strength to cross the narrow channel, white sides reflecting heat like a mirror. I climb out and walk alone, about half a block up the ditch until I can barely see them laughing. I have to jump out and paddle madly to get back across and J.D. grabs my hand as I zoom by, thank God, swinging me onto the wall so I can scramble up the bank.

We go back to the house and night comes. We're given a guest bed with a broad window behind it looking out over a cactus garden, and we sleep.

The second day we drive the truck and J.D.'s van way out into the desert in the late afternoon with piles of blankets and sleeping bags and whatever food someone grabs: hot dogs, some water, and a bag of peyote buttons. I've never seen the desert up close, and it amazes me to just drive off-road, out amongst giant boulders, really big, house-sized boulders and scrubby sage. We dump our stuff and make a ring of rocks for a campfire later. I feel like the desert is a huge room with no walls, and a tidy one—not littered. Wherever we have landed is incredibly beautiful. Each plant has a space and a place on the softly undulating carpet of hard, sparkly sand. As the peyote takes effect and the sun falls low on the horizon, the floor of the desert becomes jeweled and the plants distinguish themselves as entities to be revered, along with the smooth and noble boulders, the reddish, craggy, desert rocks that allow us to play amongst them, and we do. Hide and seek, chase and climb, flirt and rest; the evening is breezy and cooling down, and I love the desert sun and gentle air that adds to the aura of glittering and flat, spare beauty.

After eating our hot dogs, cooked quietly on a small fire, we scramble into sleeping bags. I lie in mine close to Mushy's, a bit separate from the four friends, embers now behind our heads. Humbled by the awesomeness of the huge and dome-like desert sky, I feel vulnerable as always when psychedelicized, a little nervous, and Mush is quiet. One of his duties, in my mind at least, is to bodyguard—watch over me—and to keep the other guys away even though sharing is the ultimate decorum of the group.

I'm star gazing as the planet turns under us slowly, as the zillion-star light show melts almost into my skin, then oomph—JD jumps on top of me with his golden-boy grin. Thud. What a fucking lot of nerve; I feel both compromised and uneasy. His gorgeous face is right in mine. He's every girl's surfer dream boy, but I feel fear flooding my body, triggered no doubt by other less friendly assaults. Just flings himself on me, full length, looking into my face hoping for permission, I suppose, expecting me to be all thrilled about it. He is adorably cute, but it's entirely too weird for me to imagine letting him into my bag and then into me, which without speaking, I sense is what he's asking for. I know it isn't hip to be such a sexual sissy. I turn my eyes away from

JD's questioning grin, his heavy closeness, to Mushy, lying right next to me, who doesn't flinch or utter a word. I see that it's my call; he's just watching. A trade might have been fine with him, but I don't want to. Darrell and Liz are both breathtaking: glowing, in-shape and athletic, both perfect for mini-skirts, both a little giggly and loose, silly girls who seem mindless to me. My fear is reflected in J.D.'s disappointed face. In the split second allowed for deciding on free love or not, I conclude that my body isn't mine to give just then. I'd given it up in trade for rent and groceries, a hand to hold and I want it that way. I need Mushy to anchor me. My eyes must have read like a prompter, "Get away! Fragile, do not ravish without proper approach." JD is gorgeous, but I don't want to complicate things—no desire for one more man to deal with. "Oh, OK," he replies and moves back to his bedroll between Darrell and Liz, one of whom is his for the evening.

I have succeeded in alienating myself.

The next day we all go up to Jerome, the old mining town where Barry and J.D. have a hide-out for fifteen dollars a month; the little wooden-frame house is high on the side of the hill, a rickety clapboard with a porch and outdoor plumbing and a wood-burning cook stove. Very picturesque. The mountain, Southwestern light—clear, sparkly, smell of trees, dirt, stars all in one is an introduction to life beyond the city for me, and I feel like I am walking around inside a piece of art—roads, the creek, meadows below and all.

The first morning I realize the only water on the property is the cold faucet in the kitchen. There's an outhouse in the side yard for bathroom needs beyond hand washing. I ask where people bathe when they hang out in Jerome, and they say I could wash up in the waterfall: another test. We hike up the steep road towards the summit, and everyone tells me it will be too cold in May for a bath in the thunderous pool, but they don't understand my city-girl need for cleanliness, my passion for the exquisite experience of wild water. Waist-deep next to the crushing weight of the falls, I rinse and soap and shampoo my hair that reflects sun like copper and brass mixed. The guys get to look. This much I'll grant them. When we return to the house, white-blonde, extra-tan Barry gives me his size-ten cowboy boots that are just a bit too big. I think my venture into the freezing pool so early in the morning gains me a bit of respect. I'm extremely happy to have some new old boots, and I don't care a lick that the toes are a bit too long. I do try to talk him out of turning himself in to do time in Arizona's big house, but he tells me all of life is a prison and he owes this to his parents. He feels he needs to pay for his crimes. I tell him I'd rather be outside the walls than inside regardless, but he's dedicated to cleaning himself up. Going on the lam doesn't suit him. Mushy is quite stoked to have custody of the truck, and it is no everyday kind of vehicle. It's a genuine souped-up jalopy in tiptop condition.

One of my self-assigned, unspoken duties as Mushy's old lady is to prepare tempting meals out of almost nothing: flour, beans, cornmeal, maybe fruit and meat –the basics. If I won't screw his friends, I can a least cook a few meals to earn my keep. It had to be one or the other or both, at least, in those days.

When I shop at the tiny ghost town grocery store, the large Hispanic ladies behind the counter ask my dog's name, and one clucks disapprovingly at Lucifer, my Border collie puppy. I'm wearing a white batiste dress hand-embroidered in the Philippines, and his long white fur is very complementary, but they aren't impressed.

"Hay, El Diablo!" she says, turning to her friend and rolling eyes at me as if the two of us together have a frightening significance. His name is, for me, another attempt to get a handle on what evil really is, but they don't seem to appreciate my efforts. That morning in the front bedroom, before the exodus to the waterfalls, Mushy had drawn a hexagram on my naked back and tried to exorcise my demons, the ones that cause me to retreat into myself, into moody sulks and solitudes that push him away too. Maybe the ones that had cost him a night in Liz's sleeping bag. He thinks I am possessed by something that makes me unhappy, unfree—something that keeps me from loving him, which holds back a joy that he can see in me, but that I can't let out. I appreciated the attention to my naked back, and the drawing with his pens was like a massage. He drew on me while I lounged in the lumpy bed in the little wooden house with the morning light streaming through old cotton curtains, the cook stove in the kitchen waiting for me to light it and cook breakfast for six people. It might not have been demons as much as the effort in front of me to produce grand meals for everyone on a woodstove. The women sold me eggs and bread, potatoes, juice, fruit, beans and rice for dinner, cornmeal and honey and salad makings. Several meals for all.

I don't suppose I'd be writing any of this if it weren't for the fact that Mushy tried to throw me into the Grand Canyon on the way home. And maybe he was just pissed that I got so drunk at the town Fiesta Days celebration our last night in Jerome, an annual event for the town. It was a wild party in the little strip of the Old West Main Street: chugging contests, watermelon eating, sawing logs (I lost that one). I'd climbed on stage and sung with the local jug band then went home with one and screwed him unaware that a window gave passersby a fair view of our shenanigans—Mushy was insanely annoyed. I suppose that was it— not screwing his friend but choosing to fuck a strange musician while under the influence of whiskey and beer, the two crassest of drugs. I have a definite weakness for guys who play guitars. Yeah, I admit it. That must've been why he was going to end it all, for both of us, that day in the Grand Canyon. His macho pride was hurt.

After I realize how I am in bed with a stranger and there are people outside watching through the space under the shade level with the guy's bed, I slip out the backdoor and go down the hill to find Mushy. He is smokin' mad, sitting under a tree, trying to soothe his nerves and make sense of it all. "I don't want to have anything to do with you, Pie," he says. He's been calling me Pie for ages. He likes the part about saying " . . . and every pie needs dough," when he gives me handfuls of money every now and then. "You fucked that guy and the worst part is you looked like you were liking it. And people could see from the road. God, how could you?" That is almost a non-sequitur—was I supposed to not enjoy it? Of course, I know I wasn't supposed to act like that in the first place, but there is no rulebook that I know of—I'd taken no vows of fidelity.

"Hey, I'm sorry, Marshall. I didn't know people were watching, for Christ's sake, and I was drunk, really, really drunk." I had gotten into the beer-guzzling contest and then when the band offered whiskey, I went over the edge. "I'm really sorry, Mush. I'll never see the guy again." Mushy is sitting with his arms around his legs, knees pulled up to his chin almost. Mad insulted. Trying to figure out what the heck he needs me around for. He has his sleeping bag out under the big tree at the foot of the hill where the road winds down from our house past the offensive singer's house, then down to a valley and some trees. Jerome is a village in miniature: cute, little winding dirt roads, wooden houses clinging to the side of the hill. He's too embarrassed to sleep in the house—too mad at me to take me anywhere. I am sorry. It was disgusting, what I did, but I seem to need to wreck things with booze and bad behavior every so often. I tell him he can hate me if he wants.

"Can I get my blanket and sleep next to you?" I ask him. "I don't want to have anything to do with any other people right now. I'm sorry, Mushy. I was really dumb." He says I may lie next to him but no sharing his bag. We sleep outside that night, side by side under the tree, just off the road. It doesn't matter to me, all that much, whether he forgives me or not, but I'm glad to be on my blanket with the two Mexican figures woven in, side by side, in bright colors, a pattern of how things should be.

I apologize profusely for my drunken indiscretion again when we awake in the morning, under the green canopy in the quiet mountain morning sun. As his assistant, his old lady, I rarely let my soul fly as loose as he does, with the exception of drunken behavior, but that isn't soul behavior. My indulgences of choice are generally of the baser sort: alcohol and tobacco and ice cream, with just little tokes of pot in order to be part of the crowd. His are the challenge-level drugs, the food of the Gods: mescaline, peyote, hashish, LSD, and daily marijuana. I really am too crass for Mushy Smith.

Our weekend in Jerome is Barry's last weekend as a free man, at least for a few years. He has to turn himself in which I try talking him out of. We are given, or at least Mushy is given, the incredible jalopy which Barry makes him promise not to sell, and me, I hold tight to my new boots. When they head back to Phoenix, Mushy and I strike out in the opposite direction. Three peyote buttons are a going-away gift from JD, and before we're even out of Jerome, Mushy insists that we eat them. Every day is a prayer for him it seems. Living close to the edge and outside the law, he attracts any drugs that have a medicinal effect on the psyche, always peeking into the other side by tripping on one thing or the other, driving or otherwise. He always always always is into getting high.

I have a nibble, just to be sociable, but Mushy wolfs down a whole button before we're over the mountains. This particular cactus, peyote, sacrament of the Native American Church, is innocuous looking–dark sage, a squat button like a small king's crown flecked with tufts of short spines. Its taste is famously bitter, its skin soft and wrinkled like an old person's. I know people who try smothering the flavor in a blender, making it part of a smoothie, others who dry and dice it. This morning, the buttons are fresh and insanely bitter and juicy. I gag as I try to swallow my nibble. I put the brown paper bag with the one and three-quarters of a button left over in the little black glove box.

The truck is an absolute dream. The inside is smooth and newly upholstered black leather. The gear shift is a stick that comes up out of the floor, and the engine has been replaced or rebuilt so it roars powerfully, and we are zooming up and out of Jerome, over the desert hills towards the Grand Canyon, then home to our pad in the City.

Sensory perceptions heighten as we approach the southern rim. Mushy as usual has some kind of random plan, and today's is to experience the Canyon, no preparation of course. No maps, water bottles, food, hiking gear, hats, clue as to where we are or what we're doing, just the plan to see it, the Canyon, and to be there in the existential meaning of the word. I'm into that, into just being places, dangerously close to vegetating, but an activity one can take just about anywhere with little effort or foresight.

"Hey," he says, as we pull out of sight of the little house after kisses and hugs and wishing Barry the best of luck in prison. "Hey," Mushy says. "I want to stop at the Grand Canyon and just dig it for a while, okay?"

"Yeah, I guess," I say back. We do have good directions that day and manage to get there in no time at all. The red truck likes to fly across the desert, and soon we're approaching the rim riding on our coolest of cool seats. We stop in a flat gravely area about a block back from the edge. Off-road and not in any designated lookout, there is no parking lot, no ranger or signs, no guard rails, no one in sight for about a million miles in every direction. The late morning sun is glaring and already hot. In 1968, natural wonders in America were still unfenced, often unsupervised, and almost pristine.

We amble to the edge and Mushy seems to have something in mind about getting down a bit, to climb down just twenty or so feet. We stand on the real rim, mesmerized by the Grand Canyon itself on this warm morning; just below us a grassy ledge offers a place to enjoy the spectacular view: the gorge, the sharp, jagged walls; the snaking river reflecting sky some thousands of feet or miles down. It is an easy descent to the lip of earth, which leads nowhere but to a precipitous fall. We are so alone—the only humans, birds float wide-winged in updrafts, pleasant and private. Our very own Canyon viewing. We sit facing the sun and basking like lizards. The touch of Mushy's sun-browned arm against mine and the warm air and the uniqueness of the opportunity have him, of course, leaning over me with kisses and soon enough his hand's up under my skirt. I don't mind. It feels right, like a natural part of the trip, of being high together, but I know we'll have to be careful. Often, almost always, I'm in a loose flowing skirt, making it fairly easy to screw on a slip of earth that feels like God's palm. Mushy's hand is up my thigh as he pushes me gently back with the rest of his body and gets on top of me without my giving it much thought. Just seconds into our embrace, however, I realize we are slipping and have probably lost precious inches already. Digging in with my bare heels and nudging him off of me, we sit up, closer to the edge than I want to be. With about two feet of crumbly dirt between us and the fall to certain death, it's obvious to me that losing control is too dangerous. But oddly, tall skinny Mushy with his crystal blue eyes, is entranced and sits staring now as if tired of it all, whatever "it" is: sexual rejections, societal rejections, my rejections, life's dejections. And he's maintaining an oddly firm grip on my left arm. I start edging back toward the cliff wall behind us, but he's holding my wrist, not wanting to move back with me. He rather blandly, and still in a trance-like state, to my great surprise suggests that we jump. "Pie, I want to jump," he says. "Let's just jump." I know I've heard him correctly; there is nothing but silence surrounding us, and Mushy isn't a jokester kind of guy. "Let's just jump," he says again, looking down at the tiny river miles below. He turns toward my worried face. "Come on, Pie; I think we should. Now. Let's just do it." He already has my wrist in a locked grip. I look closely at his breath and expression—dead serious. "I've always wanted to commit suicide," he says, now staring at the spectacular canyon wall across from us, "by jumping from a high place, really, and I think I'll take you with me." He says all this with just enough malevolence in his usually kind voice, that I know it is a deadly game, a for-real kind of thing. I'm hoping the new tone means I can somehow save myself, since it doesn't really seem like Mushy who is speaking. Something weird has taken hold of him, even beyond the peyote known as medicine. I surely do not hate life so much that I want to end it by jumping into the Grand Canyon with a small-time freak like Mushy Smith, nor do I really believe he does either.

The firm grasp he has on my arm is taking on new meaning, and as nicely as possible I say, "Mushy, I don't want to jump or die, so I'm heading back to the truck. Come on, Mush," as if there were really nothing so unusual in our situation, trying to sound assured and in charge. Any kind of hysterics might push him over the edge, so to speak, and I am bargaining with him for my life. He has the strength to just fling me over, and his grip on my wrist is unrelenting.

"No, I mean it, really—like a lovers' leap—just end it all now." He goes on with his proposal in the mesmerized tone, as he stares dully at the Canyon, and again how he's always wanted to kill himself by jumping from a high place and this seems like the right time.

I am edging back an inch at a time to the cliff wall and manage to lock myself against his pull, saying little stall phrases like, "Now, come on Mushy, come on now, let's just move back this way a little." He must be pretty ripped on the peyote by this time and insane and the combination isn't good. "There's no reason to jump, Mush. We didn't come here to jump, remember?" He looks at me silently, trying to remember, it seems. I am horrified of the image of myself flying to my death, or the two of us. "Let's go back to the truck," I plead, "and we'll find a place up there to get comfortable on my blanket." When in doubt, try sex—we were, after all, barely out of our teens. "I don't want to die, so let's go up and talk it over." He agrees and takes my hand as I lead him to the first step up. Once we are on the flat ground on top, and the truck is in sight, I start moving fast, pulling him with me.

"Well, I'm gonna jump anyway, Pie, I need to. I'm tired of this world and this is just what I have to do." It becomes a tug of war with our arms.

When he starts fighting my pulling hand, I remember that he has the truck keys in his pants pocket. "I'm not into suicide, so give me the keys." I release him and demand the keys, trying to be nonchalant, as if asking for the keys before he jumps is an every day thing. "It'll be a real drag if you jump off that damn cliff with the truck keys in your pocket." I put out my hand. He dangles them above my reach looking at me with a glassy-eyed grin. I walk to the truck and get my blanket out of the back.

"Look, let's just relax for a while, right here." I pat the smooth wool beside me and stretch out as if to rest in the warm sun. He sits down with the keys in his fist, and we wrestle in that crazy kind of sex play, fingers digging, until I scream and come up with the keys which I throw at the truck door.

"Okay, just let me go," he says, winded, but his mind is still on the suicidal thing. "I'll go alone; I want to jump, I have to," he says again, as if he were talking about jumping into a swimming pool. I quit holding him.

"OK, so be so stupid." I stand up and dust myself off, pretending I don't care if he jumps, walking toward the truck, bending for the keys. "Just do it," I yell at him, "I'm driving back to San Francisco, and you can just go ahead and throw yourself into the damned Grand Canyon then if you think that's such a terrific idea." I hope he won't. He kissed me on the lips when we were wrestling. I want him with me. I watch him run full tilt toward the rim, hair blowing, open shirt flapping, long legs gamboling full of life and strength. He's running fast. He stops about four feet from the jump that would have landed him rolling onto and off of the jutting lip we'd abandoned, but he stops at the edge and looks, then turns and walks back to the truck where I'm already locked in, in the driver's seat, the blanket tossed in back. As he gets close enough to the truck, I see that his face looks satisfied that he'd gone far enough. A job well done. The whole thing is just too weird, a beautiful morning gone way awry, a bad trip on peyote. In silence he stands by the shotgun door. "Are you okay now?" I ask. He nods, looking more like himself.

"I changed my mind," he says. "Let me in. Let's get outta here."

"Okay," I lean over and unlock the door, "but I'm driving to the road." He gets in and sits quietly.

We both look at the paper bag in the opened glove box, and I feel like a fool—like we've committed a sin to behave like this. "Let's bury it," I suggest. I start the engine. "Let's drive to the road and find a place to put the rest back into the earth."

"Good idea," is all he can say. Shortly after turning back onto the unpaved road and away from the Canyon, I stop the truck and Mushy scratches a shallow grave in powdery desert topsoil; he replants the sacred peyote buttons. I scoot over and let him continue to drive, satisfied that the thing is over.

We travel in stunned silence for many miles until somewhere in the mountains, he picks up a couple of hitchhikers heading for the City, San Francisco. There is really only room for two to sit in front, in the tiny cab, and I want to sleep, so I sit in back with one of them and drink a beer and feel the hot wind blow my hair around like crazy. It's too windy to talk. The day is sunny and clear, and I feel young and happy all of a sudden, and free. I wrap myself in our sleeping bag, vow to avoid peyote and high places with Mushy and snuggle down against the tailgate. The hitchhiker has the other end of the pickup bed. It's an easy ride, then, back home, to the cool fog of the Bay Area and familiar lights and city streets.

    I left Mushy when it was time for R to return to the states. The dream was real in my head, a real fantasy that burst after a few months of trying to be together in Portland.

Merimée Moffitt

Isham

From my vantage point of pulled-back, corner of curtain, the deep wooden porch was a sea of blue-shirted men, shoulders stacked like sardines from the door to the steps. Afraid they'd come around and in through the kitchen, I ran to check that door and, yeah, they were already pounding on it. "Open one of these doors, lady," he said almost politely, "or we're gonna kick 'em both in."

"Do you have a doctor with you?" I questioned. The front porch had been too close to Diane for me to talk to them. I didn't want to have a yelling conversation with her worst nightmare, the police, while she was birthing her first baby in my living room. The old wooden back door had a glass window, too; I felt the cold air coming in around the loose caulking and heard their voices quite easily. One overhead light bulb lit the drab walls of the never-remodeled Victorian kitchen, but it was mine. I was the proprietress. I paid the rent, and I knew they had no business breaking in.

"The ambulance is coming," another man answered. There were just a couple of them on the back steps.

"I'll open the front door as soon as they get here," I called attempting to sound authoritative, my face close to the window. "I'm going back to the front of the house." I surprised myself at how much I was bossing the cops around, but there were lives at stake, and I didn't trust them to be thoughtful and intelligent. Diane had looked up at me when she heard them arriving outside, so sad and scared I couldn't help but try to give her time.

"Don't let them take me," she pleaded. "They'll take my baby away."

"I don't see why they would," I said not answering the door, still stalling for the ambulance. She didn't look comforted. "I'll do what I can," I promised, as cop car after cop car pulled up in front. Luria, our pseudo-mid-wife neighbor and hippie grand dame, had insisted on calling for the ambulance from the phone booth down the street. She had delivered her own babies at home with friends, and weeks earlier, told me how simple and natural the whole process was. I'd been convinced. She promised to help Diane when her time came, but when she saw the tiny foot stepping out first, she ran to the phone booth across the street, me right behind her. "I can't do a breach birth," she'd stated, flat-out turning down the job. But she stayed with us. We came back into the house and waited.

"Look, it's not a crime to have a baby," I assured Diane. "Are you okay?" I bent over her. She looked beautiful as usual, especially in the dim light, her thick blonde hair fanned out on the pillow. She didn't seem in pain; the baby's tiny toes were just visible under Diane's raised knees. "It came so early; no one's gonna blame us." She still didn't look convinced. Two years of being a Portland runaway had added to her paranoia; she was barely seventeen. I knew nothing at that time about teenage onset schizophrenia. The banging on the front door was getting persistent and loud.

"Open up or we're gonna break your window, lady." I went back into the entry hall of the old house where John had knocked a couple of months previously and explained how Diane didn't want to get out of his car, how he was on his way to Mexico and was not taking her with him. What an incredible cop-out that was. A real local hero, dropping his pregnant and known-to-be unstable girlfriend at my house for me to deal with. It wasn't like I'd gotten her pregnant, for God fucking sakes. Not a joyous occasion, but I had told him that she could stay. What could I do? She was my friend.

"Yeah, Okay, John. There's an extra room upstairs." Diane had been sitting in the car, refusing to get out, more or less like that scene in the yard when she refused to come in. Stubborn as a goat, this Capricorn woman. As he went to the car and literally and humiliatingly dragged her up the steps to my door, I remembered the previous signs of dementia: the praying in the rain, the lurking in Miki's backroom and not coming out for weeks. Nonetheless, it didn't seem like the end of the world to have a pregnant crazy runaway teenager move into my house. There were extra rooms. The place was an old barn of a house with four bedrooms upstairs, one down, two living rooms, but it disgusted me that he'd do that. Just put her right there at the foot of the stairs inside my door, with her baskets of clothes and things, then hopped in his car and disappeared again.

She still barely looked pregnant, even the night of the birth, and I hadn't actually started getting ready except for talking to our neighbor, the proclaimed midwife, and of course Diane wouldn't go to the clinic for pre-natal, a new notion anyway in 1968. She was too afraid of being returned to her parents. What on earth had they done to her? She never did tell me—just something about violence and insanity—generalized. When the first officers answered the call about the baby just starting to pop out, feet first, I'd told them at the door they'd have to wait until the ambulance came. "She's in the middle of having the baby right now. Can anyone deliver it?"

"Well, no," one of them answered. "We'll wait for the medic to come."

"We need a doctor, not a bunch of cops to freak her out totally," I told them. "You'll have to wait on the porch since you can't do anything anyway; just wait here so she doesn't get hysterical." They said they'd wait a few minutes.

Someone had just arrived and they were making a path for him to come into the house. But he was just a superior officer.

"Okay," I said. "Just the one who will help with the baby. The rest of you have to stay outside." Fat chance. It was a cold Portland night, and by now about forty cops were falling all over themselves to storm the door, which they did, right into the sitting room where Diane lay luminous in her antique white nightgown. I'd thrown the blanket over her bent and elevated knees, but her glowing hair and belly lay odalisque-like in the dim room. Everything in the room except Diane was dark, old, antique. Her bed was near the door that opened into the entry hall and a cold gust of cops swept into the room, rushing to pack the place for the freak show.

The only light was the lamp with the silk shade we had moved to the foot of the bed so we could see the feet, the hope of live birth. The room was the original sitting room, one that opened with double wooden doors into what we called the living room. Both rooms had dark velvet curtains and ragged Oriental rugs; the lamp threw off a light that looked warm, but the men who had barged in weren't closing the door to the hallway and everything felt refrigerated. I stood beside Diane then moved behind Luria who was at her feet, so at least Diane could see my face in the crowd. Then the newly-rushed-in man was kneeling at her feet, checking the status of her delivery but he wasn't a medic—no kit, no tools, no nothing.

Diane just watched me silently as I implored the cops, "Would all of you please wait in the hall or the next room?" I asked them politely, but my voice carried no impact. They continued to creep around like navy blue cockroaches. I figured they were dying to snoop around my hippie house. Maybe they could busy themselves lifting sofa cushions and opening every container in sight. I knew the house was clean. That I was sure of since I'd just flushed our only joint down the toilet after our phone call for medical assistance. They'd said right on the phone that the police would arrive first, then an ambulance. Home births were against the law.

Luria stayed at Diane's feet. "It's okay," she said kindly. "Your baby's going to be okay. We just have to get her out now, so you're going to have to start pushing really hard." Diane's white cotton nightgown was still covering her arms and breasts and some of her belly. At least nine, black-suited men were gawking. "Push," Luria said. "Come on now, just wait til the next contraction and push really hard." Diane hadn't been doing much but occasional moans before that. There had been no warning, no nothing; she'd just appeared downstairs in her nightgown that afternoon, saying her water had broken and she thought it was time.

"Time?" I'd questioned. "Time for the baby? Oh my God." I had jumped up from reading in the only furniture in the sitting room besides a narrow, single bed. I knew nothing about birth except that it was happening right then. I could tell by her face that she wasn't wrong. It was coming.

"Lie down and don't move," I had told Diane. "I'll run and get Luria."

The baby's feet had been sticking out for at least ten minutes, it seemed to me, maybe less, maybe more. I stood behind the squatting officer and Luria had her hands on the tiny body that squirmed and twisted and was miraculously sliding out of Diane. Another cop held a flashlight to Diane's vagina and the quickly-arriving baby. The room was too cold. "Close the door!" I called to the idiot men.

Luria laid the baby on Diane's belly as I worked my way to her side again to look down at the miracle that was happening. Diane and I caught each other's eyes as she put her hands on her daughter's small, wet body.

Her high-necked nightgown fabric was between her breast and the baby's face and fists; the baby looked scrunched up like a juicy fat worm just slipped from the cocoon; her whole little self had splotches of blood and white creamy stuff; dark, wet hair on her head. Diane and I held her airborne together as Luria tied the cord in two places then I snipped it with scissors someone had magically come up with. The officer stood watching—the men were milling about the room, continually opening the front door to blasts of Portland night air.

Someone must have whisked the placenta into a convenient bag. The baby wasn't doing anything—no sounds, no cries or breathing. "I think her airway is clogged with mucus," Luria said, "and I don't have a syringe. You'll have suck on her nose and mouth to see if you can help her breathe." No time to lose, to argue or panic, and Luria said, "Merimee, just do it" and by God, I did; within seconds of cutting the cord, in one motion I lifted the tiny body up to my face and as if kissing her, sucked gently on her nose and mouth together, maybe the way cats do it for kittens, somehow it seemed reasonable and natural—praying to God that I'd know how to do this thing that women must've done for each other for millions of years. It worked. She gasped.

The doors opened again: more men and a stretcher. A medic finally knelt at Diane's feet and proclaimed she looked okay but would have to transport to the hospital for immediate medical procedures and blah-blah-blah. The baby was still naked in my arms, gurgling and breathing. I was trying to give her my body heat; someone handed me a small blanket. The stretcher guys were focused on taking Diane away, already, telling her to scoot and slide and not allowing time to lift her gown to nurse. Nursing a baby in those days was also suspect behavior, I suppose, not too far down the list from flag burning, the crime of shoulder-length hair on men, refusing to kill in Viet Nam, etc. After forcing Diane onto the cot-like stretcher, the gawking doofus next to me opened his hands indicating I was expected to turn over the illegal goods: the baby. Then he insisted. I couldn't believe they were taking mother and child to the hospital so quickly; that they weren't waiting to do it right.

"You need to have some kind of wrapping on the baby." I had her still wrapped in my arms, pointing out the obvious—naked, one thin blanket—and we had nothing nearby; it had all happened so fast. "It's freezing out there," I explained, nodding to the windows, astonished that they were so intent on possession of the baby that they showed little concern for her protection from the elements. One guy had another small cotton thing they'd brought in from the ambulance, and they draped it around her, insisting that I hand her over. There was nothing more than two receiving blankets loosely swathed around the newborn child when the morons whisked her into the night, and I watched them go. I hadn't fought hard enough; I'd acquiesced too easily, too silently, still stuck in the manner of the fine education I'd received, the fine upbringing of being a good and cooperative female.

"Why are you taking her?" I asked the stragglers, meaning Diane of course, but not wanting to say her name.

"Routine procedure, lady. She may need a couple of stitches and she has to be examined."

Diane, on the stretcher, followed her daughter to the ambulance. No one had asked my name or numbers. They knew I had no phone. They had their prey, the criminal baby-birther.

"You'll be fine. They'll let you go, don't worry," I'd said to her as they rushed her out into the night. I made no promises to follow her. I had no car. I didn't want to be questioned. She was living under my roof and harboring a runaway was still a crime. I simply closed the door.

Several years passed before I saw Diane again. She called me from the coast when she heard I'd moved back to Eugene from Taos with my young son, about Isham's death; at four years old, the baby Isham had gotten into some neighbors' overflowing septic tank mess and had come down with a terrible fever. "It's probably for the best, though," Diane said sadly. "She was never quite right. Life was a struggle for her. She was very slow."

I went to visit John and Diane, together now for seven years, at their house on Alsea Bay. When we arrived, I was immediately enchanted with Diane's life and hippie abundance, in spite of a missing tooth that I didn't ask about. John had taken up carpentry to support his family, and a huge yellow school bus was tucked up against the shrubs and vines in their driveway. Diane gave me a tour of the bus which was in the process of becoming their new mobile home. There were tables and beds and cupboards in various stages of installation. They would be going to John's grandmother's house, Diane said, as the landlord of their rental was reclaiming the property. Inside, while John and the poet and Davy the harp player plucked and crooned some blues, Diane showed me shelves stacked deep with canned fruits, jams, sauces, and home-made berry wine in deep purple jars. Her face glowed with pride, and she had no problem collaring my wild-child son who was playing too roughly with her sweet little towhead girls: Freya, and Nephele and Hannah, all about the same age as my son. Diane's choice of names gave a depth and sense of pride and history to the family background she had refused to divulge while still a runaway and desperada. I was impressed.

In the back room she had a treadle sewing machine, and she showed me some muslin skirts that would go up for sale alongside the others in the shop in town. At least some of the time, between bouts of the madness that would ultimately seize her, she had been happy.

Hey Hippie, El Rito 1970

Greta Golden was my friend in the City and in Portland where she'd changed gigs from erotic-movie model to macrobiotic fanatic. Greta had social skills and always had artists and musicians drifting in and out of her domestic scene. Tidy, 1920s style furnishings and kitchen stuff and her pretty, German-hausfrau smile welcomed one and all to come on in. I could drop into her soirées with impunity, get high, have tea or food, visit a while, then move on. That's what we did in those days. With no cash for most events, we ourselves were the events and our bodies and homes were decorated sets ready for whatever drama would unfold.

Smelly was how I wound up in New Mexico. We were both at Greta's on SW 1st Street in Portland one rainy night, and I was headed home to my empty house across town because George and I had ended our brief and erroneous marriage. I hate to say pathetic because it sheds such a poor light on my own judgment, but that's what my marriage to George really was: pathetic. From my point of view now, I'd say George was kind to take me in out of the weather—I was on the rebound from my failed plans to marry Randy. That had all gone south mostly due to my fixation with the Irish poet, who never committed to anyone. He was an addict to the core; heroin his only true love.

I'd heard direct quotes on the grapevine after I married George that people pitied him. I was a viper, gossip had it, who'd simply play with him a while then swallow him whole. But I didn't feel that way about George; we'd had a relationship looking to happen, a very short marriage of sorts as if that might cause a connection, but it didn't. I don't know why he didn't tell me to get the hell out of his life and house, but he didn't. He was a gentleman albeit a bit of a thief and a drug addict.

Smelly hit on me a month or two after George disappeared south in the spring of 1970. I was planting an ambitious vegetable garden (in George's abandoned scene), working my dead-end job as an artists' model at the Portland Museum Art School—an existence totally on the fringe, and that's where I found my friends too, like Smelly, who was sitting on Greta's floor one night due to some rather strong pot. I was on my way out the door and noticed him in the entry hall, alone, sort of sprawled against the wall as if life had flung him there, and he'd slid down into the most comfortable position. He grinned and said, "Take me home with you and I'll cure your blahs."

I wasn't sure I'd heard him right, since it was such a direct and audacious come-on; nothing had led up to it that I could recollect.

"What?" I queried, just to make sure I was actually being offered a romp in the hay. I'd barely even spoken to the guy. "Take me home with you," he repeated, smiling a kind of curled-mustache, Al Capone smile, "and I'll cure your blahs."

Well, I was impressed that a guy who hardly knew me would notice that I had the blahs; I, myself, hadn't thought about having blahs until he'd mentioned it. My self-esteem wasn't so intact, at that point, that I could separate having blahs from me being blah. His comment implied to me not only that he thought I was worth a fuck, but also that he thought I had a curable case of something; I didn't really care if it was blahs, depression, insanity, whatever. The fact that he found me worth saving, fixing and saving, attempting to save—even if only for the possible pleasure of sleeping with me at least once—well, I found that intriguing.

"OK." And that's how it started, me in New Mexico, Michael, our son, my life. Smelly and I caught the late bus home; I hadn't had wheels since George left, and Smelly traveled light. Sitting on the bus, lightly touching at the shoulder, I felt like I had a date for a show we were both looking forward to. He needed a place to sleep besides Greta Golden's sofa, and I was very curious about the "blahs" thing, often taking people at their word.

When we got to my little bungalow, I wasn't really nervous. Smelly and I'd been around each other on the scene before: parties, dances, dark corners of dark houses. He was friends with friends of friends from Seattle, vets on the rebound, lots of drugs and not much coping with the hell their lives had turned into due to the big boys in DC with the too much time and money on their hands. Smelly was a connection, I suppose. He had managed to wheedle out of Nam, exactly what I would've done myself. I admired the guys who had the foresight not to go, and he was one of many who simply connected the drugs from supplier to user, keeping his customers happy, collecting his fees and moving on.

We undressed in my big front room/bedroom without touching or kissing. This was clearly not about love or an undying passion for each other. This was naughty sex, experimental. Like, what exactly happens when you get into bed with a guy from nowhere who says he'll cure your blahs? The street lights lit him partially as he undressed by the heavy double doors that separated the old sitting room from the living room. My double bed faced a ground-level bay window where damask curtains let in a sliver of light. We faced each other across the bed and climbed in. He was sweetly plump and white with a dark pony-tail half-way down his back and enough black hair across his chest and arms to seem manly.

I knew I had nothing to lose, no face to save or not save. Not tall or big enough to be overwhelming, Smelly's body was comfortable and didn't smell bad at all. He was smooth. We lay together under blankets on clean white sheets and he caressed me, waited to feel responses, sex in more of a "Mother-May-I?" game form than I was used to. Steve had fucked me like Thor the Thunder God, for years, eventually leaving me crazy and bored; then Mushy, whom I had used for room and board but loved in a funny, non-connected way; then Randy, who was too crazy/kind, strange/demented, normal/beautiful; and the poet, ah the poet. The poet had abandoned me for his own madness and addiction. Then George. And George just didn't work out. That's not such a long list for a twenty-four year-old make-love-not-war goddess.

Smelly had me interested in his appreciative way of making love. Blahs gone. Bingo. Confident, non-pathetic, not even a whiff of neurosis, just easy-going animal pleasure. Simple, slow, patient. I liked things plain and simple. I felt like he really enjoyed the company of my voluptuous body, me; he ran his fingers up and down curves, then in the long clinch: "I love the feel of you getting off."

"Nice!" I thought. I was so stoked that he paid enough attention to me to feel what was happening and didn't beg the issue of quantifying my orgasm. A lot of previous experience with egomaniacs who pleased themselves first and foremost, then demanded that I speak of my pleasure in their performance, had me somewhat apprehensive. Some had demanded nothing and given less. Always convoluted. Always fucked up, and of course, endless rounds of pot and beer and whatever else always messed up my mind so I hardly knew my tail from theirs. Did I come? Was it good? Hell if I knew; most of the time it was more like a fast ride up a bumpy dirt road on an old Harley than goodness, except with the poet. But with Smelly, it was easy; he was reading my relaxed body like an electrician closing all the connections, one by one: hip, nipple, thighs, back, shoulder, arms, neck, and chin, then plug in his tool. Yeah, this works. Satisfaction. I would've followed him anywhere.

Before sleeping for a while, he invited me to come with him to New Mexico, a trip already in the works. "Hey, I'm going to New Mexico next week. Wanna come?"

"What're you gonna do there?" He was lying on his back with one arm behind his head; the other held a cigarette.

"Nothin, just hang for a while. The guys have a house they're going to they had last summer. I'm gonna check it out. You should come." Blahs cured plus an adventure. Not bad I thought.

"Okay," I agreed. "When?" My first trip across New Mexico years before hadn't counted as anything more than a brush with disaster, but the open desert, the endless expanse of space and sky stuck in my mind as worth investigating. There must be something going on there that attracted all these people from the Northwest.

I had friends living in El Rito, which at the time had a teachers' school where my friend Dennis was getting a degree. Miki, his artistic wife, always ran a nice hippy home, open, inviting, food on the stove wherever she lived. I knew I'd be a welcome face at her door. I thought it would be just fine to hitch a ride with Smelly and his buddies even though he warned me I could bring only what could fit under the front seat and one backpack of belongings. I'd go hang with Dennis and Miki and check out this New Mexico scene that had kept them busy now for a while. Smelly would be a great ride. After we slept awhile, he split in the morning light, saying they'd be back in a week or so to pick me up.

Smelly's real name was James, but no one called him James or Jim. He was an okay looking guy: dark, long hair slicked back like a turn-of-the-century Sicilian, not tall enough to be intimidating but not short, not fat or thin, neither built nor flabby, not smart or dumb, no career or education, no talents or job, but not a beggar; he was clever enough to hustle a meager living without getting caught. He liked to get high and to get his friends high, so small-change dealing and hanging with the guys for a good time was what he did. His name and come-on were unique; his easy ways and touch of bad-boy self-confidence made me feel equal, no needy kind of second-class-citizen-ness spell that large men held over me. Large men in my life had a way of making me so dependent that I'd cook and clean and cater to their needs just often enough to get laid, but not often enough to get married, or be satisfied. But Smelly, aka James, and I, had no delusions between us, ever, that there'd be a lasting connection. We were both along for the ride, and I knew he'd dump me the minute I became extra baggage.

"He was caught sniffing underwear," the friend in El Rito told me, the big friend who was on a dole from grandma and would go back to straight school and life very shortly if he didn't die first. Smelly was the kind of guy who slept alone often, on sofas, in corners on a sleeping bag, in the back seats of cars. His better-looking friends would have a bed and girls in bed with them. Smelly picked up leftovers, rejects, rebounds, and had been caught one morning standing in the middle of a bedroom sniffing the crotch of someone else's girl's panties. "Just seeing how they smelled," he said, hence the name. I didn't care. The trip to El Rito with him was a one-wayer, but I didn't mind because I fell in love with the turquoise skies on the very first day.

When Smelly's friends with the big old shiny-green Chrysler pulled up at my house, I was ready with my cast-iron frying pan, my best cooking utensils, a backpack full of clothes and jewelry, a sleeping bag, and Tonga, my white and ragged, standard-sized poodle. All other possessions had gone in a yard sale which left me about $100 to start a new life with in New Mexico. Smelly's friends in the car groaned because there were already three people and a dog. With me and Smelly and Tonga there'd be five adults and two dogs, but they all relented when I promised to pay for two tanks of gas and take only the kitchen stuff that would fit under the seats. Tonga would sleep on my feet, I promised; we climbed in back and were off for a non-stop haul from Portland, Oregon, to El Rito, New Mexico. Rotating drivers made it an easy one day, one night drive. Smelly and Tonga and I switched to the front seat, shotgun, sometime after midnight. "Hey," he said. "Come 'ere."

"What?" I asked to his whispered query. He was pressing on my shoulder. The blonde, guy friend was driving, in his own world; the car was quiet. There was plenty of room on the big front seat for me to slip down a bit and do the deed. Hmmm, so much for sensitivity, I thought, feeling a bit used; but then again, I decided he deserved it, getting me the ride and all. I was aware I didn't have the nerve to say no, to be so uncool as to say no, also aware of how I felt—that he wasn't very cool to even ask me to do that in the front seat, in the middle of the night, with his friend driving. But it was nothing to get all bummed about, not really a big deal. Guys were guys, and sex was sex. Stuff like this happens.

I took the wheel somewhere in Arizona near dawn and knew then that I was having fun, in spite of the rude blow job. No blahs. And nothing quite like eating a green chile and bologna sandwich for breakfast as the sun rises over an Arizona horizon.

"What? You've never had green chile before?" Smelly was incredulous as we pulled into the parking lot. It was like, where had I been? I was a green chile virgin at the age of twenty-four, but not for long. The parking lot where we stopped was gritty, the store funky, the sun really bright and hot at dawn. We all made sandwiches—white bread, bologna, green chile bits lifted out of a small can and spread on the bologna, eating slouched in various stages of somnolence, yet my body felt alert in the clear desert air; the sharp, starkness of dry desert was welcoming me to a new home and the outrageous flavor of vitamin C-packed chile. We kept the Chrysler still for the bathroom/food break as I stretched my bare leg out the driver's door, already working on a tan, feeling sexy, alive, still curious about where we were going and what I'd find.

Smelly's two guy-friends were vets, recently home from Nam, no jobs except to be on the dole and get high. Foods stamps, crazy money from Uncle Sam, whatever mom and dad would fork over. The girlfriend was a Seattle chick who liked drugs and guys who liked drugs. Within two years, the young Marilyn Monroe cheerleader type would be dead, floating drowned in her parents' bathtub at home in Seattle, OD'd. That would sadden and surprise all of us horribly. How could she have been so stupid as to get hooked on heroin, then take too much before a nice hot bath? So sad; so pretty and young. You'd never have guessed. But that was a winter or two after our trip together.

The old adobe in El Rito was a drying-out, trying to stay alive, twenty-dollar-a-month, low-income asylum for these crazies and their friends, or so they said. Next door was supposed to be a kind of high-class moonlight ranch with cowgirl hookers, but the fields and fences between us were such that I never got a good look. The supposed hookers had their own weird world. Our place was a two-story adobe, old, old, with a genuine single-seater outhouse and a Snow White kind of well. There was already a little garden starting up which had to be bucket watered. The driveway from the road was one of those long, bumpy, adobe alleys between fields edged with barbed wire fences, double rutted with native grasses and weeds along the sides, about three lots long then a parking spot by the well and the kitchen door in back of the house.

Michael Troxel lived downstairs with his girl friend Cathy and Cathy's daughter. He greeted us as we pulled up—standing six-three in sandals, rolling a smoke, smiling. Everyone loved everyone here, it seemed, all hugs and slaps with Michael and Cathy who'd apparently arrived weeks before and set up the house, planted the kitchen garden.

I marveled at the brightness of the light, the hard-packed adobe yard with the adorable old well and mini-garden next to it, planted in the pale soil. We, the weary travelers, entered the kitchen through a door frame older than my grandmother, a threshold eighteen inches deep framed in weathered two by twelves, gray and dry and curling on the edges. The three rooms downstairs were all deep adobe, impenetrable by bullets or sun or any vibration. The kitchen had tall-paned windows set into the walls, and an old white-enameled wood-burning cook stove that sat on curved and gleaming chrome legs. The floor boards had shrunk over the years to leave gaps wide enough for dirt to make a dusty grout. I was utterly charmed by all of it. The other two rooms on the first floor had such small windows that kerosene lamps were lit even during the day. Michael and Cathy and the little girl occupied the biggest room downstairs, so I didn't really get much of a look. It was their bedroom.

    The kitchen was the gathering spot for the household, a picnic table with benches in the center, a couple of rickety oak chairs by the windows. The house had never been wired or plumbed; a wide shelf along one wall held two gray-enameled dish pans. Beneath the counter was a galvanized bucket to carry in the water, filled outside from the well bucket. I went back out with one of Smelly's friends, the blonde guy with the ponytail to get a drink, and he showed me how to crank up the bucket. I was in love with this place already. A soup ladle hung from a nail on one of the posts that also held the rope and pulley. When the bucket came up, he told me just set it on the wall and use the ladle to get drinks. Leftover water went into the little patch of lettuce plants. I drank, then watched the darkened rivulets roll along the rows of tiny lettuces just poking up from the undernourished golden-colored soil. Everything outside was brilliantly lit by clear skies, a close sun. Inside was a cool cave.

The afternoon I arrived with Smelly and his friends from Seattle, I set my things in the upstairs room allotted to the two of us. I was his old lady at least temporarily, as I tacitly understood the arrangement, our relationship infantile in more than one way, but so far decent enough, a terrific ride, identified and removed blahs, a new pad, a new state. I didn't mind. Not bad for a pickup off Greta Golden's floor. Smelly announced to Michael as we entered the kitchen, "Hey, not only do I have an old lady, but she's got a summer-weight down bag." I laughed inside that my cheap little down sleeping bag was something for him to brag to the guys about—and set just about equal to my being a new old lady, also noting that I'd met the handsome Michael Troxel before, in Seattle, on some sofa where he was talking a minor drug exchange, and I'd been observing his long legs, back then, one ankle resting on a knee, his hands behind his head, relaxed; his were the bluest of turquoise-blue eyes I'd ever seen.

One deep-set window in our upstairs room, framed in old wood with a coat of chipped, sky-colored paint, looked out on hills speckled with piñons and sage, a diorama lit up in the afternoon sun. Cottonwoods rustled down by the river just a field or two away behind the house, the only sound besides birds through the open window and murmurs from inside the house as each couple settled in. I laid my jewels out on the sill: earrings, necklaces of Venetian beads, a Tibetan safety pin, an ivory elephant brooch found by George at the Portland city dump. On a piece of silk on the board floor, I extended the display of my worldly goods whose glitter would comfort me. There was no furniture. The room, in contrast to the gloom downstairs, was light-filled. The tall sash windows on both the east and the west sides, standing just inches up from the floor, provided direct and indirect sunlight that filled the room and turned the floorboards a dull grey. The walls were flawed white wash over old adobe. I rolled out my Indian blanket, then Smelly's bag, with mine opened on top as a quilt. The room itself was an antique gem. The stairs, without a railing or banister, opened from the floor of our room down into the dark end of the kitchen below.

Smelly was smoking and talking with Michael and the guys, and I had a strong desire to be alone after the twenty-four hour stint in the Chrysler—wanted to explore my new surroundings, so radically different from the streets of Portland and West Coast vistas I'd grown up with.

The long driveway led out to the road, into Carson National Forest a mile or two up the slope if one turned right, or if left, into the village of El Rito. I stood outside the house, deciding which way to head. The forest was visible in the distance where the valley of golden grassy fields ended abruptly and a wall of evergreens started, opening only to let in the highway and whoever traveled on it. After announcing I was going for a walk, I headed out the driveway and started the hike to the tall woods a mile or more away. I had an hour or two of sunlight left. No one wore watches or owned a clock that I knew of.

Apparently the local welcoming committee had seen me on my way up the slope, Red Riding Hood-esque, and must have licked their wolfish chops at the prospect. I had noticed them cruise by—white car low to the ground, four dark heads—as I hiked along the shoulder of the road towards the forest. At the top of the valley, the golden colors of the grasses and fields changed abruptly to shadow, green trees, fairly dense tall pines. I hadn't much desire to walk farther in than the first glimpse and sensation of damper, cooler air, so I turned to head back, totally enjoying the vista from the glade's edge. The dotted and curvaceous hills to the left glowed almost pink in reflected afternoon sun, and every tree and bush in each field seemed distinct in the clear desert air. The wide, deep-blue sky capped the entire valley as the sun nudged towards the horizon on my right side. The road back to our driveway was a long ribbon, bordered on both sides with quiet land.

About half-way there, the guys in the white car returned, this time cruising down the right-hand lane, slowing their pace to match mine as I walked on the left side facing traffic, but there were no other cars. I increased my gait to maximum speed as I scanned the fields for hope of some help; the four leering faces checking me out knew exactly who lived where and maybe exactly how many people would not be around to rescue me. I remembered then how the road was desolate, devoid of houses, only cows and a lonely horse within sight, and one small white building set back off the road, so far away it looked like a Monopoly piece. I picked up my pace. The one small building was my only hope if these guys really meant business; they were rolling along beside me, seemingly ready to pounce.

"Hey Hippie, " the dark-haired driver started the conversation in a taunting tone. "Where you from?" I didn't answer. I glanced into the car and saw their faces laughing at me, four grins devoid of any humor I could relate to.

"Oregon," I said holding my head up high, and walking as fast as possible without seeming to run. Chin up, I thought to myself, and walk fast. Get ready to run. But not yet. If I ran, they'd chase immediately and attack.

"Whatcha doin' here, Hippie? Hey, wanna fuck me, Baby?" the same one asked. I looked at him briefly, with a faint smile as if acknowledging a joke. Ah, yes, very funny. They all laughed with bared teeth and open mouths. The fear in my gut stayed put because I knew I had to bluff, had to edge closer to my only hope of help. They all four had dark eyes and none of them looked like they really cared who I was or like they could see me at all. They thought they knew what I was, hippie pussy, and they were getting excited, mad, it seemed; another outsider invading their little community that they wanted the hell out of so badly, bored as they obviously were. I had a fleeting vision of my body bruised and mangled up in the field after these guys were through with me; my pace still matched the car's until the driver wrenched the wheel towards me, my cue to break into my best run as he opened his door towards me and got out all at the same time. I didn't run often, but I knew I needed immediate rescue; my body was electrified with fear. As his foot hit the pavement, mine crossed in front of his car towards the driveway of the tiny house, still barely visible.

Blessedly, unbelievably, I saw a woman waving at me from behind a vehicle parked in front of the house. They must have seen her, too, because they stopped the car and waited at the foot of the long dirt passage which had an open gate. As I got close enough to focus, I became aware that the thugs were waiting on the road to see what was going on. She waved me up her adobe driveway, and I arrived panting and gasping. She opened the shot gun door of an old tan pickup parked by her back porch. "Come on," she said, a young woman about my age with a dark braid down her back over a vest and shirt. She was wearing snug tan jeans and spoke English with a touch of a Spanish accent.

"They did the same thing to me once," she said as she climbed in on the driver's side then backed out of her dirt road with confidence, raising dust as she careened backwards onto the road and slammed into gear, a clear communication to the wolves in the low rider. "They're not nice boys," was all she added. She gave me her profile only. "Where are you going?" she asked. "I saw you walking up the road to the forest and I've been watching for you to come back. I saw them, too." By this time they were right on her bumper, but she stayed in the middle of the two-lane road. If the welcome wagon boys were allowed to pass us, I sensed, and she must have too, they might run us into the ditch. They tried to get around on her left but she wouldn't let them; she just swerved as they did and kept them behind us. She didn't say any more. When she turned down our driveway, they kept going into town.

Everyone in the house came out to see who was getting out of the truck, but she didn't look at them or let go of the wheel, just let me climb out as I mumbled a thanks, then threw it in reverse. I never saw her again.

Smelly made a show of getting a gun and finding the guys who had scared me, but it was just a show. He turned to Michael who stood behind him in the doorway, "Hey Michael, you got a gun, man? I'm going after those assholes."

"Nothing happened; I'm okay," I assured him. It would only escalate and get worse if we did anything at all. He needn't die for the insult to all of us. I promised to walk with Michael's German Shepard, Sol, next time, or with a gun or both, and the incident blew over.

It was only a matter of hours into the third morning of our stay when Smelly announced to me quietly that he'd be leaving for the coast with some friends who were coming through. There was no invitation for me and I didn't ask. Honor among thieves; I wouldn't disgrace or sour our perfect little escapade. The game of life we all played simply unfolded as it told itself, and I'd known he was just a ride. He said he was sure it was okay for me to stick around the hacienda for a while or hitch a ride out whenever I wanted; later, there'd be people coming and going. Basically, I was free to make what I wanted out of what was in front of me, and I decided I'd visit Dennis and Miki to see what was happening with them.

In El Rito, there was a small college called the Normal School then, just west of the tiny main street which sported a couple of art galleries and an old adobe restaurant with a walled garden where I'd seen the owner lady outside hitting flies with a swatter. Smelly's big friend with the Grandma money waited in the car while I went into the P.O. to ask about Dennis and Miki, to find out if they were still around. The postmaster said they'd moved to Taos a while back. "I think he graduated and got a job teaching there," the little old man told me. So the friend and I went down to the store that had wide wooden steps leading up to an ancient adobe storefront. The glass windows were held in with narrow wooden strips, also painted the ubiquitous turquoise, pale and chipping in the soon-to-be-broiling dry heat. Oiled board floors muffled our footsteps inside where two elderly ladies behind the counter stopped their talking to look at us disapprovingly. We went to the standing refrigerator for cheese and tortillas. There was a pot of pintos simmering on the woodstove at home, redolent with garlic and onions—a trick Miki had taught me in Portland which she had learned from an old woman in Nevada. By dinner time, the beans would be tender in an opaque juice, ready to fill many stomachs. "Do you have any Bugler?" I asked the senora, seeing only the dry flaky Bull Durham tobacco in pouches, tiny muslin bags with yellow drawstrings. Better than nothing, but Bugler was so much more palatable. Ready rolls were way out of our price range.

"Yes," she replied slowly, with a Spanish accent. "On the other shelf over there," staring at me as if she'd learn about my problems if she looked hard enough. The other one just stood there, arms folded across her bosom. They were my mother's age, but so entirely different, not locked into their ranch-style home, not waiting for a man to come home at five and okay the first drinks which Mother would then pour into matching tumblers sitting side by side on the apricot-colored

Formica. Daddy had somehow forbidden Mother to drink before five. But these women had a store to run in the very bright New Mexico light. Every strand of their silky black hair, every crease on their soft cheeks, seemed to be theirs and no one else's. I was terrified, way too shy to speak to these Rocks of Gibraltar-like women beyond the need for tobacco.

So Smelly split, no regrets, caught his early morning ride that came through out of nowhere and whisked him away. Within a day of his departure, Cathy's ex-husband showed up to fetch her and her daughter. Apparently Michael had just borrowed them for awhile, which had to be more than a coincidence. Michael's old lady and her daughter had been dismissed—gone now—with all their things in a truck, headed home to California. Nothing overtly unfriendly, it seemed; they had hugged goodbye and finished throwing things in the ex's truck as I watched from a corner of the kitchen. The ex pretty much kept his head down, face hidden by a cowboy hat, skinny legs in tight jeans—a nice enough guy, to come get her like that. "Well, that's a coincidence that they both left at the same time," I commented to Michael, after the dust settled, as he was headed into his dark room.

"Yeah," he answered slowly, tweaking his thick mustache a bit. "She called him a couple of days ago. Things weren't working out with us." I didn't respond, just let it go.

Still early enough to hitch to Taos. Michael alone now, watched, leaning against the doorframe as I laced up knee-high moccasins and smoothed my short, white-with-blue-polka-dots slinky dress over matching skin-tight pants. I knew my new tan looked great in this outfit I'd made before leaving Portland. It was stretchy fabric, a polyester knit affair that served as both outer and underwear since the top was fitted with elastic under my 38 C breasts, and the pants were pull-on with elastic waist, legs tucked into my moccasins. Total comfort. I had no money for clothes or underwear, so I made things from remnant scraps and Goodwill curtains, whatever seemed attractive and supple, and cheap—dirt cheap was the requirement. I'd been making things for friends too and for a little head shop in Portland, but my sewing machine had gone at the yard sale. The white with polka dots ensemble was my last creation until I scored a new machine somewhere. "Where're you going?" he asked.

"Taos," I replied. "I'll be back in a day or two. Think my things'll be okay?"

"Hey," he smiled. "I'm not going anywhere."

Michael

"Okay, well, see you then." I broke the rule about not going out alone, but it was morning and bright, gloriously New Mexico bright; I walked down to El Rito central, the village crossroads, to hitch up to Taos on the highway. There was certainly no place for fear or a dog or a gun on this trip. The visibility along the road was good; I could run, hide, whatever if someone came I didn't want to talk to. I wouldn't feel alone—too excited about the visit and the view—I was falling in love with New Mexico. Hitch-hiking rule number two: never get into cars with more than one person, certainly not more than one man. A single driver can do only so much while zooming along. If I let things like that bother me, I'd never get to go anywhere. Rule number one? Watch out!

I was back to El Rito in a couple of days, totally convinced that New Mexico was my new home, like coming home at last. Dennis and Miki had an incredible place in Arroyo Hondo just north of Taos: an old two-story adobe, sans running water or electricity, but on a hillside with trees and a well. Miki already had her kitchen garden knee high and chickens in a coop, fruit on her trees, and a bevy of kids swarming around in and out of the house. Rides had been easy, coming and going, and the countryside of desert mountains, farmland, the Rio Grande gorge—every place—beautiful. Clean air, quiet, and a visible history with a palpable sense of roots in the community that Miki was making her own. She appeared born into the generations of locals who built strong adobes and cooked with wood and hauled water in buckets from hand-dug wells. It was heaven and I loved it. The sky was a constant brilliant blue: pale in the morning, deepening hues through the day, and no rain or clouds yet for the entire time since I'd hopped into the Chrysler from the sidewalk in Portland. I was madly in love with a state, the state of being en Nuevo Mexico.

Changing clothes when he called me, I wasn't surprised or afraid: "Merimee, are you up there?" I peered over the edge of the stairs into the darker kitchen below. He was standing below, awaiting my permission to enter: my room, my body, my life, my history in the making. Did he know he'd be the father of my first child? Not likely. I didn't either, but there was no sense of choice inside me. I was his from the get-go, from the first time I'd ever seen him really, back in Seattle on a sofa next to me, in a room full of people at a party. He'd been married then. "Can I come up?" he asked.

Now this was a man with a body, a physique, a presence, and a sense of self-preservation that masqueraded as self-possession. There were no other lovers around, not our ex's or the other couple who lived downstairs. Nothing but the ghosts of the years of living and struggling that must have gone on in this second story, light-filled, adobe room. Michael stretched out on my bedroll as I sat down beside him, and then it was all so simple and easy. Not to have made love to Michael, right then, in the light that bounced off gray wood, my jewels spread on the cloth in the windowsill—not to have made love to his long lovely body would have been like passing up the tree full of fruit when Eve was told to walk on by. "Do not eat the apples," God had warned Eve, and my warning went just as unheeded.

He was interesting in his voice, his body movements, also, slow and sure. But we were almost strangers, and the unity of belonging to the same crowd of desperadoes didn't quite erase the distance that naturally hovered between us—a chick vs. guy kind of sentiment. Nonetheless, our bodies pressed together and we got busy before even making coffee or going for a walk. Looking back on it all, I have to assume I was not only numb to my own body, but also dumb to any voice of reason—a sexual mute. Sex was so often a sort of full body handshake for me in my "Free Love" period, an introduction to what might follow if we, the participants, and the rest of the universe were willing. And this time I was willing. I was mad about this guy from forever ago when we'd sat next to each other on that sofa in Seattle. He just turned me on, no particular rhyme or reason. Just the way he was—his turquoise eyes, arrogant swagger, totally non-fake bad-boy lifestyle. Michael was for real a fixer-upper's dream and a caretaker's pot of gold, not that I understood those inclinations at the time. A long, tall, white kid who had grown up on the streets of Oakland, his upbringing was quite different from mine. His friends' mothers took him in, but he bounced along from one family to the next after his grandfather died, never knowing his own father who was a father by sperm donation only, a sailor on leave, his mother a teenager who tried for three years, then left him with her father. I didn't understand at all the depths of differences between us, or that we would have a child but not be able to mend and blend our own histories tight enough to hold our family together. At first, I had no notion that I ought to care about where we came from. Beats and hippies, to me, were about reveling in the now—who we were right then, living in the now, the moment.

    And so we made love that first day, alone together in the lovely, gray-walled upstairs room with the sun falling in long rays across us. It was mellow to me, not a hot fire, but I enjoyed his body being next to mine, holding me. "Hey, you don't really get down that much, do you?' he asked, smoking now, lying on his back on my double-size bedroll. I felt the comment as a put-down, a first punch meant to put me in my place; he hadn't been that pleased with what I'd given him, apparently, my style of surrender or whatever it was that had just happened. But that's where my numbness shield paralyzed my own common sense. I so often had to deflect or absorb illogical behavior from my alcoholic parents; insults had become the norm for me. A very slick way of his taking the upper hand—putting me on the defensive. It wasn't a mortal blow, just an introduction to who he thought he was and how he thought things would go down—him in charge, me his underling. As a street survivor—he needed to be in charge or die, or get the crap whupped out of him. So he let me know he'd had better sex elsewhere, and I didn't show him the door. I took the bait and set out to prove to him my worth and lovability.

"Lots of times," I said, "fucking just doesn't do it for me." Looking back now, that comment was pure insult too, a match made in hell. I suppose the attraction was mutual instinct. What I didn't know was that there was no way we could make everything okay for each other in some kind of pleasant way—it was going to be fallen angels clawing every step of the way to ground level. I could feel myself being pushed away, some strange mental power of his to attract and push away simultaneously; I filed the comments to mull over later, justified to myself: just a small hurt, a minor set back in the bantering that I hoped would go on a long time. I liked him anyway. Hah! What a fool I was, but there was so much learning to be gleaned.

And those big, turquoise eyes; he was beautiful. Why was he in New Mexico? Who was he? Who was I? We talked about what our plans were, and that I didn't really have anything going except looking for a scene. He asked me if I wanted to go up the mountain to Vallecitos with him.

"I've got a gig rolling logs at the mill in Cañoncito," he said, arm tucked under his head, lazily blowing smoke toward the ceiling, picking loose flakes off his tongue, the tobacco that hand-rolled cigarettes always drop; "Starts next week." I wanted to be his old lady. I wanted him to want me, and here he was, inviting me to go with him to find a place to live in Vallecitos, a little town not too far from El Rito.

"Yeah, I'll go with you," I said, as if the plan had been scripted for me. To live alone without a man just didn't appeal, and I was entirely interested in hanging with this handsome drying-out addict from the streets of California, Seattle, the West Coast drug scenes.

"Why are you here, in El Rito?" I asked him, lying by his side, excited that there was at least a promise of time to be spent with him. His hair was light brown, thin and wavy with some pre-mature gray, long enough to sweep back behind his ears and down his neck an inch or two. At thirty-four he already had smile wrinkles around his eyes, and his very prominent Russian nose was in keeping with his story about his grandfather coming from Russia. Michael looked Cossack and ruthless. He said he was kicking a heroin habit, and the cops had been hot on his tail for dealing; it was get out of California or get arrested.

He talked about how he grew up playing outside his grandfather's bar in Oakland. "The only white kid in the neighborhood," he said. His grandfather had owned a small tavern with a pool table. We were still stretched out on my bedroll.

"My gramps had a cool place though; I could go in the bar any time and get a sandwich and the rest of the time I'd just run the streets. Everyone else had to go in at a certain time, but not me." He smiled at the image the memory evoked. We put on clothes then lay back down to talk.

"So you just kind of ran wild?" I asked him, seeing the streets at sundown and all the other kids leaving a kick-the-can game to go home for dinner, but Michael's gramps still had hours and hours to go before closing time.

"Yeah, but it was pretty cool," he said. "The other kids' mothers would call them, but I could do what I wanted." Michael's deep voice was so sexy I was dying inside. "We had a big vegetable garden that my grandfather was really proud of—grew damn near all our food, all kinds of veggies and lettuces." He picked tobacco off his tongue. "It was all okay until he died, and the state got everything." I became aware of our bodies stretched out side by side, and that he was making no move to love me up again. I ran my hand along his chest.

"Well, what happened to you when he died? How old were you?"

It turns out Michael was only twelve when his grandfather had a massive heart attack or something like that, and everything Michael knew was gone, instantly—house, garden, bar, Grandpa—all of it. His aunt took him for a while, he said, but she thought Michael was getting too intimate with her daughter, so she turned him over to foster care. After several moves, new families, he wound up in Korea behind a gun in a trench, at seventeen, just after knocking over a grocery store and getting very caught, very fast. Before he was even eighteen, he was in military prison for decking a snotty officer in a bar and when he came home, well, he didn't say, but I assumed that that was when the drugs and dealing set in. He later showed me pictures of a very pretty wife and the exotic girl friend who'd followed her in his line of significant women. His wife had left him; the pretty girlfriend, too.

The meadow just north of Vallecitos was our first home. Michael would get picked up in the morning to go roll logs at the little mill in Cañoncito. We'd have the truck running as soon as there was money, but we got dropped in the meadow—squatting like gypsies. Our two dogs got along fine. Sol the Wonder Dog, Michael's German Sheppard was no doubt top dog, and Tonga was my shadow, always. Wherever I went he simply followed or waited. We walked our earthly possessions through a couple of pastures, learning quickly how to get through barbed wire without ripping skin and clothes, camping in a natural clearing very close to the small river that meandered idyllically, flat and curvy through a wooded glade, grassy banks on each side. There were tall skinny trees at the back of the clearing, Aspens or Birch, that worked well for putting up plastic under which we spread Michael's nine sheepskins for our bed. I don't know why he had nine sheepskins but he did, and he was proud of them too. His iron bed and treadle sewing machine were stashed at Sandy and Denny's. The plan was loosely that we'd get a house as soon as we could. We dug a fire pit and set up rocks and a grill in our kitchen area out in the open, covered his trunk and my pack with plastic, and then walked back into town to party with his friends who owned half of an old one-story adobe. Two local brothers had inherited their family home, the one they'd been born and raised in no doubt, but only one would sell, so one end remained vacant and unused. Dark-haired Sandy and her boyfriend Denny from Seattle owned the three rooms that constituted their house. Sandy's step-sister, light-haired Sandy, and her truck-driving husband owned the house next door, and that sister would be the first woman for whom Michael would betray me.

Before we'd even left that upstairs room in El Rito, Michael had gotten me to promise fidelity. He made eye contact so there'd be no misunderstanding. "I'll mess you up if I find you with anyone else," he said, and I liked it. New, novel, and I liked that kind of clarity. "You gonna be my old lady," he said, "there won't be any others on the side." It wasn't posed as a choice or a question.

"Not a problem, but what about you? You have to commit too. It can't be one-sided"; but of course, I was silly to think that it couldn't be one-sided. Where Michael had grown up, well, everywhere in those days and it was just beginning to dawn on me, the men had different rules from their women—and I had no idea about any of that Oakland-type behavior, Michael, the only white kid in an all-black, poor neighborhood. A verbal commitment was a contract just short of marriage in my mind. I promised. I'd never promised anyone anything, and I liked my promise; I meant it and felt it. We had tied moccasins and boots and finished the fine tuning of getting dressed, and I liked the way he'd said "old lady" and how he had a clear picture of wanting me to be only his, all his. And I didn't care about my fidelity. I'd had a fair share of messing around and had no one else in mind. I told him that I could do it: he'd be my one and only. No one else had ever thought to exact such a promise from me. He said he'd be true, too, in a mumbled sort of perfunctory sentence, but to me it was a lifeline of sorts, a rope I could grasp, a new idea and tool to use in the weirdness of relationship. He told me later he'd wanted me for himself from the second I'd stepped out of the green Chrysler on my first afternoon in New Mexico. Well, really, why I thought that meant more than a farmer calling his pigs to trough was what I'd come to New Mexico to find out.

My days in the meadow were spent anticipating Michael's return from the mill and all the needs and demands that he'd bring with him. Laundry we had to do in Española, and shopping too, but with a stash of rice, beans, flour, cheese, butter, red chile, and our interesting burlap sack filled with blue corn still on the husk, we could eat for weeks without having to shop. There was a little store right in Vallecitos, too, that had a few necessaries, on the opposite end of the street from the post office—the two businesses open and running on the only street that wasn't a dirt path accessing dirt driveways. Later on I'd discover Willie and her warm tortillas, eggs from her year-round hen house, and fresh goat cheese most of the time. She must have approved of the dozen or so hippies who had moved into Vallecitos, replacing the steady drain of the local young people who only wanted out as fast as they could to get to the cities. Willie ran the tightest ship in town, lived alone, and her house looked like her parents had built and furnished it round the turn of the century. After we moved to the cabin, I'd walk the two miles into town to buy supplies from her, and she even agreed to teach me her secrets for fabulous soft white tortillas.

While still in the meadow, cowboy coffee and eggs and toast on the grill weren't too tricky to get together before Michael left for the mill. After that, I'd read, bead on leather pouches, clean up the bed and clothes, fix beans and make some kind of bread or tortillas. I learned that English muffins did cook pretty well on smoldering coals in my big cast iron pan with the cast iron grill as a lid. These two pans were the sole survivors of my years in Portland since Smelly had let me slide them under the front seat upon leaving my last Portland house. The evening before the accident I served Michael muffins with butter and honey. In the shady glen by the river, beavers were at work on a damn and a zillion birds lived in the little Eden that must have belonged to someone. It never occurred to me to care or worry about who owned the place. We weren't hurting it. We never got run off, but then again we didn't stay that long. A few times we heard local kids giggling in the trees as they spied on us. We must have been quite a sight, a fantasy encampment, refugees from the Coast. The locals just let us be, probably knowing a helluva lot more than we did about how we wouldn't be staying very long.

Smelly was back in town after a quick run to California, and an almost fight broke out between him and Michael at the first Friday paycheck party. My vows of fidelity were tested when Michael went on the beer run with the guys, and Smelly walked me onto the back porch and tried to get into my pants, steering me into some kind of big closet space. He lay us down on top of burlap sacks, but I only allowed one kiss, and it wasn't difficult at all to tell him there'd be no more available at any time in the foreseeable future. I was feeling elevated, as if I'd achieved the first level of my new game, at least. But he was pissed and wasn't going to let me go to Michael without some show of resentment. I suppose he had hoped to find me waiting for him, missing him.

"Hey, I see you shaved your moustache," he said to Michael in the eating room as soon as the beer-run guys returned. A large table was covered with pots and bowls for helping oneself. We were at Phil and Maryanne's house and the sun was just going down. The room fell silent. This wasn't going to be a peace and love kind of thing. These guys were drinkers and druggers, not thinkers dedicated to social change. Several of us were standing around the well-cooked pintos, bags of chips, beer cans, and empty salad bowl. Four paned windows sat deep in adobe walls, opening to the yards both front and back of the house—a pleasant dining room.

"Yeah, what of it," Michael said. Everyone looked around and noticed the posturing. Michael's voice was far from friendly, and he had a weird grin on his face. I'd never had anyone fight over me before, but it seemed pretty stupid that either of them should get hurt. Smelly had split without regrets or a claim on me. It would've been more thrilling if it hadn't been so obvious that messing with Michael was like teasing a rattlesnake.

Smelly didn't seem to care. "Well, you look a little bit like a frog now," he sniggered to himself, looking to us all for some kind of support which he didn't get. A guy named Drone, (suitably nicknamed as he had successfully avoided working since returning from Nam) interfered and reached out for Michael's arm: "Hey Michael, man, take it easy." Michael was an old dude who had, after all, snatched Smelly's left-over snatch, barely waiting for it to cool, but Michael was pissed that Smelly would dare to insult his looks. Smelly was on the rough pine-board floor butt first and fast, looking up and hoping to ward off a full kick to his kisser as Michael said, "Yeah, and I've got big frog legs to kick your ass with too," and at that point friends intervened with arms out and "cool-down" comments, and Smelly was up and dusting off his honor as the moment passed without bloodshed.

By the second Friday night paycheck party, the always-impending disaster was on us. Michael and I got along easy, maybe too easy. Not enough fire between us to keep him on the edge he was used to, maybe. It was another orgy of food and beer and booze and weed at the little house in Vallecitos proper. This adobe had cost the owners five hundred dollars, with ditch rights, but there was no running water. A lot of peeing in their yard at night as the outhouse was too far to walk to made their yard smell really bad. A pickup was backed up in front, and Michael and I were heading home to the meadow with Sol and Tonga when a couple of guys started collecting for a final beer run. "Hey, you wanna come along for the ride?" Michael asked me, already hopping over the tailgate. Sol landed gracefully next to him—Sol the wonder dog, pedigreed descendent of Rin Tin Tin Michael had told me; God, I'd believe anything in those days, but Sol was elegant and gorgeous, much like Michael. The night sky was dark and clear and the air perfect, a no-need-for-even-a-sweater, New Mexico summer night.

Vallecitos is at the top of the mountains; the tiny village of La Madera nestled below at the opening of the valley, which leads to Ojo Caliente and Española. Michael told me the view of the moon was better from where he was sitting, with his back to the cab, but I missed the tender gesture until thinking about it later, one of the very few he'd make like that in our seven-year relationship, but maybe I fared better from where I was when the truck rolled. The bar was closed, of course, but Mañuel would sell from his house about ten miles down the well-paved, very curvy mountain road to the closed bar. We made it about half way. I was feeling the truck struggle to keep its wheels flat on the turns. When the lurches came harder, I pounded on the cab window, but our driver was grinning and oblivious. Didn't hear me, didn't care—a drunk young man having fun playing trucks. The shotgun rider was bracing his hands on the roof of the cab. I turned and nestled down with Sol and Tonga. "Well, I'd just as soon die with you guys as with anyone, I suppose," I whispered into Sol's thick fur and held him close as the event occurred. Sol went flying; I went flying; Michael and the wood heat stove that was in the back with us went flying. We must've arced out like marbles tossed from a hand into the bushes when Mother Superior used to confiscate the contraband marbles. The truck spun and flipped and amazingly righted after dumping out its cargo. I could see the gravel on the shoulder of the road and the ravine dropping sharply to my left as I came in for a landing like a plane with no landing gear, flying parallel to the ground, skidding. I had lost consciousness momentarily. Tonga was right there as usual.

"Hello?" Just quiet when I pulled my face up. At eye level on the pavement, I saw Michael stretched out on his back. The wood heat stove, the long low kind that held a washtub on two burners and was good for taking big pieces of wood, was on its side. We were evenly distributed. Sol was standing by Michael, dark and still, almost like a cartoon with birds tweeting, but the wreck must've scared the birds. Not a tweet to be heard. "Hey," I said, "can you hear me?" I wasn't sure if I or anyone was dead.

"I can hear you," Michael answered, "but I can't move. Are you okay?" I lifted my head up, hands still flat on the dirt. The cobra position. Grit, dirt and blood mixed on my face; the front of my dress was torn and hanging, and my naked breasts were scratched but no noticeable chunks were missing. There was a pain in my back but not bad enough to keep me from continuing to ease onto my knees then stand, dusting off gravel bits, holding my dress front up with one hand. The truck, though I had seen it roll, was on all four tires, sideways across the road not too far away. It had flung us, spun, and rolled one full circle. Both driver and shotgun rider were standing looking towards us in the moonlight.

I often figured that it took Michael's broken bones and my snapped rib to slow me down enough for conception to occur.

Living on dark-haired Sandy's extra mattress for a few days in her extra room made life and Michael so unattractive I almost split in the next car leaving for the City. But Michael asked me to stay. It would take him six weeks to heal from the four broken ribs and snapped collarbone. I was putty in his hands really; all he had to do was ask, and I capitulated, recommitted myself to devotion, helping, doling out Sandy's stash of Darvon, walking to the meadow and bringing back our few valuables. The sheepskins had already diminished to two; the thieves had kindly left us one each. Bending to get through barbed wire was so excruciating with my snapped rib that I didn't return for all of it. We had to find a house now for Michael to recuperate in, and it had to be free or almost free. At least we knew our parameters. Someone told Michael about Geronimo's cabin in the valley down the road from the town—a couple miles by road, about a mile's walk if one followed the river trail through the gorge. Michael hobbled over to Geronimo's and made a deal as soon as he could stand on his feet long enough to do so.

My commitment to stay was sincere. His five or six broken bones had him laid up, and he wanted me to help him. Seemed reasonable—that he wanted me was interesting. I was willing.

The Cabin

The cabin had been a communal growers' shack, a place to get in out of torrential rains in the little valley just south of the town of Vallecitos. The farmers in town had used hand-hewn logs, a heavy wooden door, a board floor, and two windows that may have seen glass at the turn of the century, but previous tenants had tacked in murky plastic that slipped its frame and wasn't quite air tight. The ceiling was traditional: vigas and latillas made a roof with three inches of dirt and small rocks piled on top. Not much dust and dirt sifted through the closely-laid poles (latillas) laid crosswise on top of the peeled and oiled vigas, but just enough onto the bed so that in the morning I would throw back the covers and sweep the bottom sheet before pulling up the top sheet and quilt. The cabin was as old as the oldest people in the village, or older. They had used it before statehood, before losing the land grants, before powdered milk and food stamps replaced growing vegetables and raising flocks and herds.

Michael had a Morris chair with dark velvet cushions and a standing lamp with a silk lampshade that he'd brought from Berkeley, along with his treadle Singer sewing machine that he'd used to make leather hats. Ah, my new sewing machine. There wasn't any electricity, so the lamp was just decoration. The place came with a small but curvaceous wood cook stove, complete with a warming oven and well-fitting circular burners that could be lifted with the lifter tool in order to poke a slow fire. Stove wood was shoved in through the little door under the burners; that fire box was our only source of heat and energy, other than our bodies.

It was June when we moved in, and Geronimo, the town elder, charged us fifteen dollars a month to be the sole inhabitants of the entire valley, a fee he promised to waive if Michael would take care of his old horse for him. Neither of us had the faintest notion about horses, but we promised to toss the animal some hay and keep an eye out as it wandered around the tiny meadow beside the cabin and the fields that sloped from the irrigation ditch in front of the cabin to the river, two or three field lengths across the tiny valley, one vallecito in a string of many. There was no outhouse, so we designated a section of field unused for anything else, for an open-air toilet just like the cows and horses, grateful that the snow and ice would mix it all up then fertilize the fields. No one seemed to care and there was no one around except the occasionally snooping landlord or one of his ancient cousins. Sometimes we saw the little bear scurrying up the hill just across the rutted road that led down from the paved road to our little hideaway. We could hear any vehicle coming to the cabin or the valley of pastures long before they actually pulled up to our pile of firewood.

Geronimo was a cool old guy, cool because his wife Amalia and house in Vallecitos were tidy and proud, and he let us live in his cabin. He had brought us a sheep when the weather started getting cold and he realized we were planning on settling in for the winter; he and Michael butchered it in the tiny clearing by the cabin. We were surprised and pleased when he gave us half and told us to keep the rapidly freezing chunks in the blue trunk on the north side of the house with the snow packed up around; it kept just right and fed us for months. Geronimo, who had timed that slaughter perfectly, knew how much the half a lamb would come in handy, especially if the weather got really bad, and it did. At eight thousand feet or so, the winter was for real, and that winter was an especially cold one.

Geronimo was cool also because he kept his ninety-year-old mother in his house with him, and I loved to see her from the doorway when I went to pay our rent (fifteen dollars a month) during the late summer and early fall while the mill was still running, when we had an income and before he brought his horse down. (He only left the horse a couple of weeks until he fully understood the depth of our ignorance about horses.) His old mother would shuffle across the kitchen with her tatting in her hand, doing a step-slide, step-slide, so free and easy—the way any old person would want to be rather than in a hospital full of pale flesh heaped in wheel chairs. I was impressed with the arrangement. This old woman was still making things and being part of her family. I liked Geronimo a lot for that, even if his wife didn't invite me in.

I didn't mind that Geronimo came to the cabin when he knew Michael wasn't around and asked me to walk out into the fields with him, to check on his cows. He flirted but he never got too pushy; I liked how he could take no for an answer, and I knew I could outrun him or his horny old cousin, maybe even just tip them over like cows—they were that old.

The cousin did come down one day to have a chat with me in front of the cabin, making me very aware of how alone we were. He asked me if he could come with a bunch of his cousins and rape me some night, and I was pleased to say that this cousin also took no for an answer. That one puzzled me. Was he serious? Was it a way around the rules? He also warned me that we had to have enough wood, a lot more than we had, or we'd freeze to death.

I never realized that Michael was screwing around in town with Sandy's step-sister light-haired Sandy until Denny showed up one afternoon, wanting to get it on with me. Then I knew. He was letting me know that I could even the score with Michael, and easily, right then. It was almost a point of honor and his respect for me that he would make such an offer, but I had made vows to Michael and even his disappearing for two days and Denny showing up didn't make me want to break my vows. I was getting attached to Michael. I liked him. I liked our life together. I liked living in the valley.

The first morning of that winter's cold snap, January 1971, I opened the wooden door, and the plastic

Free Love, Free Fall

one which Michael had built to give the cabin more light, and stepped out to pee on the hard earth that sloped into the ditch just yards from our threshold.

"Hey, Michael," I called into the cabin, pulling up grayish-white long john bottoms. (I did laundry by hand in buckets of heated-up river water between trips to the laundromat an hour away in Española.) "The thermometer says thirty-seven below; Jesus!" I shivered and decided to get inside before my bare feet did some act of disconnection from my still-warm body. The ten-gallon milk can that held our drinking water inside the cabin had popped its little top and leaned like the tower of Pizza. "Hey, the can's so frozen the bottom has bowled out"; I rocked the can on what seemed to be a pregnant base. Michael, under the pile of quilts and down sleeping bags wiggled his shoulder. It was gorgeous cold. The entire brightly-lit valley was frozen solid. I turned on the radio and the voice was admonishing parents to not let their kids wait at the bus stop. Even in the sun it was thirty-seven below.

"Are you gonna build a fire?" he asked. "Make some coffee." It wasn't an unpleasant demand. Coffee was my main drug in those days. The mill had closed already for the few months of below freezing days.

Sitting on the edge of the Morris chair, I pulled on socks, green wool, foot sweaters I'd knit as thick as little jackets. The chair faced the valley, visible through the flimsy solar door which the sun had not yet hit. I tied two rabbit furs around my wool socks, making impromptu slippers, then hopped around in the crisp January air, opened the fire box and cleared the grate.

My breath was making noticeably solid white clouds, inside the house. It had been so incredibly hot when we first moved in the previous June, we'd never really sealed the flapping plastic windows around the bottom corners, figuring a little fresh air wouldn't hurt us. Some of the logs had enough chinking missing so you could actually see slivers of daylight between them, reflecting off the trees behind the cabin. Fall had been a dazzle of colors as the scrub oak, cottonwoods, sugar pines, and piñons prepared themselves for winter. I'd done some watercolors and sent them home to Mother and Daddy. We'd put in a pile of squaw wood and mill scraps that would have to be replenished, but it didn't take much to heat a tiny cabin. I knew we had enough wood to make it for a while, but I also sensed that no matter what we did, it would be tricky to get the cabin above freezing that morning; it might take hours.

I hopped up and down getting the kindling going, then bigger pieces, then a couple of chunks of piñon that would burn for an hour, eventually poured water for cowboy coffee into the blue enamel coffee pot. It was still entirely too cold inside to do anything but climb back into bed seeking body heat from Michael.

Those six days were too cold for walking, and no chance the truck would start. Mostly we read and took turns stoking the fire and fixing little meals. More of the water finally melted in the can. I must have stayed horizontal long enough for the little starter sperm to meet with its starter egg. My first baby. The news on our battery-operated radio said people up and down the mountain had lost cows and horses on the first night of the cold-snap when it dropped to forty-seven below. Geronimo had long since taken his old mare back into town.

We had agreed that getting pregnant would be okay: it must have been some survival instinct set off by the isolation of living in the valley alone, some innate tendency to want to fill space with humans—it certainly wasn't logical or well planned. I was having the biological urge to procreate. Michael, looked at me the night I said, "I thin I'd like to get pregnant. What do you think?"

"I'd like that," he said, and that was about all it took. I always had the Pollyanna-ish notion that things would work out—there would be a way. He had a job, I loved the little village, maybe we, too, could buy a house. I didn't have an exact plan, nor did he share one with me, but we needed each other to survive that very cold week, and I believe that's when our son was conceived.

Michael liked that I decided to stay with him, and that our togetherness led to a baby in me, but he would turn his back in bed as if I were a bore so many nights—I began to feel he didn't like me. Then the disappearing into town for hours, sometimes days, leaving me alone. Never sincere apologies or real explanations and I was feeling smaller and smaller—didn't really know what to do. When he got violent, I was already looking for a way to exit—to get some relief from his condescension, his continual mood swings and belittlements. By the time I knew he was not going to be committed to me, I was already pregnant. I'm guessing now that he was doing more than womanizing. Once an addict, always an addict, but I had no idea at the time. Still don't know for sure, since all those people have disappeared or died several years ago.

And I liked being pregnant. Full and with a purpose. Spring had sprung. The mill up the mountain in Cañon was open again; Michael went back to work rolling logs from the stack to the saw, stack to the saw, stack to the saw. He used a long metal bar to pry them loose, aimed them at the arms of the machine that would hold them in place for peeling and slicing, and then paychecks, again, every Friday.

One particular morning in April, I stood at the open cabin doors, my tummy rounded and smooth, firm and convex. Michael was tying his boots as I relished the warm air filled with alfalfa smells and the earth and pine needles from the trees behind the cabin. The valley between us and the river was already warming up—the last seasons' grasses crispy dry. The walk to the river was three long fields, two barbed wire fences, and uphill all the way back. My belly said, "Don't do it. Don't carry the heavy buckets up the hill. Ask him to do it." He had enough time before he had to leave for work.

"Do you think you could go get water for dishes before you go?" He looked at me like even looking at me was a chore. He had to work for "the man." I would be in the cabin all day, or somewhere in the valley or in town. My time was my own. All I really had to do was clean up and somehow produce the evening meal—be pretty and useful, plentiful, and agreeable.

"I'll do it when I get home," he answered. "You have some drinking water." The dish pan was piled with dirty dishes. I hadn't washed my body for days. I really needed water.

"I need it now and I might lose the baby if I do it," I said, feeling my voice go whiney and anger starting a power surge inside me. I was entirely and immediately pissed that he didn't understand that I needed water, and in those days I had no leash on my own feelings. They came and went like natural weather. I'd miscarried Randy's baby the year before, and my body was sure that I shouldn't carry heavy loads up a hill. I felt crazy with rage that he sat there resting, despising me for needing him to carry water.

"Goddammit," I screamed losing my temper entirely, very quickly. "I don't see why you can't just go get the fucking water for me? Is it really all that much to ask?" There wasn't a shred of humor in me—nor had he displayed any humor about me and our life in the cabin. It just wasn't funny to either of us. I wanted things my way and knew nothing other than screaming like a baby to express myself. This just unglued him totally. Do we hate most the weaknesses in others that remind us of our own? There was no mercy. It pissed him off that I was pissed off. Neither of us knew how to relate to another's needs—how to use patience when love demanded patience. We didn't know. The rage in my body was so powerful I needed to throw something, anything to make the anger bearable, as if the anger itself would sail across the room and splat against the logs and chinking along with the half-full pot of warm coffee I'd picked up; grounds and coffee dripped down my neck from my stupidly spilling it on myself before the blue metal pot crashed into the corner, not anywhere near where Michael still sat in the Morris chair. I laughed at myself with the coffee all over my long johns and the wall, but there was no humor in Michael's need to control my pressure-cooker feelings. I didn't much care that I'd just given myself another chore to do. I did all the housework anyway, but Michael seemed to care that I'd vented by making such a mess, and he entirely cared that I was raging at him—pregnant or not. If I was acting like the nasty-tempered lioness in the zoo, he rose to the occasion and claimed his dominant position. Jumping up, his hand swooped under my arm and sailed me across the room like a big Raggedy Ann doll before the coffee grounds made their final kerplop. I fell on the bed screaming as he jerked me back up and slammed me into the plastic door.

"Oh, big tough guy's gonna throw me around a bit?" I was terrified. I hadn't thrown the damn coffee at him. I went to the bed and sat with my head down, hoping to God he wasn't going to knock my teeth out. "I'm leaving you," I said. "This isn't working out."

"Good," he spat back. "I'll help you get a ride." He went off to work angry, and I made the decision to leave him. I found my own ride. The only thing I could do with my confused feelings was to run, to separate from him. Perhaps I needed to find out what was him and what was me. Perhaps I was putting my foot out to start on my journey of self-discovery. I wasn't really aware that running and hiding from just about everything was a pattern we had in common.

George Louis, who lived with his wife and son in La Madera, was going to California. Louie, we all called him. Louie asked me if I'd like to ride out on the back of his Harley. He wanted to take his Harley to San Francisco, and he would love to have me behind him, he said, gallantly, hoping I suppose, that I was the kind of girl who would swoon over an offer to ride bitch across country on a very pretty Harley with a sweet long-haired guy in leathers driving me into the sunset. I guessed it was an offer that might even bump his wife out of position, but I wasn't interested. That I might lose the baby was all I could think of. I needed a ride in a vehicle not on one, so I declined Louie's first offer, but at this point I was ready for pay backs: sex with someone who actually claimed to like me. When Louie let me know he'd decided to leave his Harley and catch a ride in our friends' van, I accepted.

It was early May when Michael dropped me at Louie's house, just a year since I'd shown up in El Rito, and now I was almost five months pregnant. Michael followed us to the La Madera store where I stayed in the van, sitting primly on an upturned milk crate, watching his broad-shouldered back. If I'd gotten out and followed him into the store, things might have taken a different turn. But I sat tight and watched his handsome swaggering self stroll into the Mercantile for tobacco. We didn't even acknowledge each other. Years and years later, on his death bed actually, Michael admitted he'd followed us to the store to try to get me to stay that day, but then he didn't say anything. He'd simply let me see him walk into the store; if I'd gotten out and begged him to keep me, well, maybe he would've. But there was no begging in me. I had no other way to cope with the full picture: pregnant, the cabin, a violent man, not much choice for me but running while I could. I must have needed to go to Eugene, and it would be over a year before I returned with our son.

I rode out from La Madera in the van with Louie headed to Yosemite. Louie wanted me to be his old lady, he said, but it was a no-go. I was tired of new guys. We made love in the van somewhere before Yosemite and again that night in the campgrounds, and I liked Louie but he was married. I didn't have the passion for him that undoing and re-doing his life and mine would require. He was just a nice lover, a nice guy. Michael was already in my blood, and I longed for him by the end of the first week of our separation. I wanted him so badly to follow me and find me, rescue me, love me. By that time, I was in San Francisco longing for him almost every day. We weren't really through, but he didn't show up. He didn't call or answer my letters sent from my girl friend's house. I headed home to Mother and Oregon where I got on welfare, food stamps, and pre-natal care and hoped for the best. He didn't call until the night I was at my mother's house and in labor. She had said she'd drive me to the hospital. I lived alone and didn't have a car. Amos was born in Eugene, Oregon, in September of 1971. After delivery, I awoke in the unwed mother's wing of Sacred Heart Hospital. The nursing nun in flowing white habit told me, when I asked where I was, that they'd moved me to "the unwed mother's wing," she said, "so you won't feel bad when all the husbands come in to visit." That was 1971.

On the way from the delivery room back to my special wing of shame, I saw my brother sitting for me, waiting to see my face. We gave each other wan smiles. It had been a hard labor for which I was mightily unprepared. My gay brother, pre-gay lib, pre-coming out, was my best pal and support though he was more clueless than I. We at least knew we loved each other, and I had achieved a new title—unwed mother. My baby was healthy and adorable—red-cheeked and a screamer.

Merimée Moffitt

Learning to Speak Up, Out, and Over the Edge

We were dirt poor—almost literally. The two-room cabin must have been one of the original adobes in Talpa, New Mexico, just a few miles south of Taos. Talpa was and still is a community of houses, small farms, and an elementary school all tucked into rutted and winding dirt roads at the southern-most base of the Sangre de Cristo Mountains. I fell in love with Taos and its surrounding villages from the moment I arrived in hopes of reuniting with Michael—we would give it another try at being a family. He had come to Eugene when our baby was six months old and spent a month hanging out with us. When he got back to Taos, he worked for a friend doing electrical and got together enough for me to buy a plane ticket.

    Almost entirely old adobe buildings and pot-holed roads slick as snot when wet, Taos was the most mysterious and different city I'd ever seen, sitting at 7300 feet between the majestic mountains on the east and the sweeping mesa to the west that sprawled, gashed by the Rio Grande, as far as the eye could see. I'd grown up all over the West Coast as my father sought his fortune in the lumber industry, never establishing deep roots, never even noticing deep roots and the people who had them. In Taos, there seemed to be room for a few more misfits and desperadoes, a welcome as tangible as the tumbleweeds.

I was fully hippie at that point in my life—handmade clothes, my baby in tie-dyed diapers, no straight job, no property, nothing tight on my body, beads and quills, bare feet or moccasins, all home-made. Ethnic and macrobiotic foods plus Alta Dena ice cream, of course, and the pace in Taos was slow, manageable, sane. From the moment the big Greyhound bus pulled up in front of the one-room station with a dirt lot, I was newly at home on the planet in a place that may not have changed very much at all through World Wars I and II, Korea, Nam, the 50s, the 60s, and Civil Rights. I hadn't yet heard of the Women's Movement. It took my first *Ms.* to wake me up to the reality, the possibility, of sisterhood.

When Michael sent me the money order to get a ticket, a woman friend who lived upstairs in a garret apartment had been evicted with her two baby girls. She was sleeping in a park, and thinking she needed the money more than I needed a plane ticket, I gave her the money to rent a place. I wrote back to Michael and a few weeks later, he sent me more, but not quite enough to get to Albuquerque. I'd have to fly into Denver and catch a bus to Taos. The day the bus pulled into Taos, was an exciting day for me, not only was I so excited to see Michael, who had his good qualities and his friendly smile waiting for me, but also because Taos was amazing. The bus curved down the only paved road so close to an adobe wall made out of old mocha bricks that had been laid to curve also. I was in an old city where an ancient culture blended with descendents from Spain and Mexico, and gallery fronts were filled with paintings and pots, jewelry, leather works, Martha's dresses, everything local and impressive. The light in Taos is magical, and I sensed, on that very first day, that every day in Taos would be a beautiful one. The day I arrived with my nine-month-old baby, I fell in love, not with a man so much, but with a place.

Michael had found us a two-room adobe in Talpa, a place next to his boss's house. He would work as an electrician's helper, and I would set up house and let my life unfold day by day. The place had a really horrid outhouse, but we had bathroom and laundry room privileges next door. Our little adobe house was primitive but cozy with a woodstove and plenty of space for our meager belongings. And life proceeded, and I had a daddy for my baby, and we didn't really talk much about our future. Taking care of the baby, focused on the basics, we existed in a somewhat amicable togetherness.

In the fall, Michael was laid off, and it fell to me to find a job. I was ready to get out of the house a little more, and our neighbor told me that the new community pool couldn't open until they found a swimming teacher. Their funds were tied to educating the local school kids in the fine art of swimming (rather than drowning in ditches), but no one had even applied. I was a strong swimmer, loved the water, and thought, what the heck? I can teach kids what I know, having had a couple of sets of lessons, I wasn't afraid to try anyway.

There was one certified lifeguard (and eventually another) and a helper boy. That was it. The plan was to bring in busloads of kids from all over the county, and I'd teach them to swim. I may have gotten the job due to the homemade bathing suit I'd thrown together, but I did swim all the strokes across the pool and back as per instructed. I told my new boss, however, that I wasn't a lifeguard. My teaching plan satisfied his inquiry, but I insisted that he or another lifeguard would have to be present while I instructed. The job lasted several months until that one day, a big boy drifted into the deep water just as the lifeguard stepped into his office. The kid was fine, but it could have be death if he hadn't heard me screaming over the din of some thirty kids in the huge pool. And all the while, Michael was home when I was working.

It does, in retrospect, seem that he had kindled a relationship with my one friend we'd met while in Vallecitos, whose husband had left her with a child Amos's age. Her name was Kelly and she was an heiress, a nurse (unemployed), pretty, and skinny. Eventually, she would come between me and Michael.

He started disappearing on weekends, not coming home to me often enough that I figured he was out tom-catting around. I dropped by her house one afternoon to ask her if she knew who he was seeing. "Me," she said, challenging me beyond my limit.

"You?" was all I could say, then tears all over me as I put Amos back into his carrier and onto my back. I wouldn't look at her or even speak until I'd confronted Michael and he was very much not giving her up.

"We can have an open relationship if you want," was his solution to my outrage. "But I'm going to be spending half my time with her. You can go out with whomever you want, too." But I only wanted him, and I wanted her for my friend.

On the day of the first *Ms.* magazine, I'd just gotten home from downtown Taos where I'd scored the absolutely coolest cookie jar, and the new magazine for women that didn't look at all like *Cosmo* or *Seventeen*. Having always been a reader, I planned on devouring every article as soon as the baby was asleep.

It was a sunny spring day in 1972; Michael was back at work with his boss, and I'd taken some grocery money, Michael's old truck, and the baby, and had gone down to the Plaza. Every Northern New Mexican village is centered on a plaza—a small square park, usually with a raised and covered gazebo and a lovely adobe church on or near the square. A dime store, a drug store, the mercantile, an art gallery, one clothing store, three bars, and the La Fonda Hotel with its paintings by D.H. Lawrence lined the sidewalks. I don't recall exactly what I was looking for by wandering into the dark mercantile with the oiled wood floors. My baby was in his pack on my back, and I probably wanted to lull him to sleep before the ride home. In those days, without car seats or seat belts, laying a sleeping child across the seat was the smoothest transition to home, at least with my wild child.

The man in Gabe's Mercantile told me The Humpty Dumpty cookie jar had "sat on the shelf for at least twenty-five years." No one wanted him because he'd fallen and had been glued back together, but I was enchanted. He sat alone, too, at the end of a long, half-empty shelf. The store looked like business had been slow for a decade or two. I could see the darkened seam along Humpty's chubby shin and rounded shoe, tucked under his egg-like body. The crack and the patching only made him more precious to me, and at $2.50, I knew he was meant to be mine. Cookie baking was one of my wifely skills, no matter if I had to split the wood myself. On the counter near the cash register sat a stack of the new *Ms.* magazines. I'd heard the term *Ms.* in Oregon and how savvy women refused to be called Miss or Missus any more, what with no male term to match the subtly sexist differentiation. *Ms.* seemed like a gorgeous assertion of independence—a "Why do you need to know if I'm married, anyway? If I need you to know I'll let you know." I hadn't had a chance to use it yet, being dropped out, counter culture and career-less, but I loved it—the notion of deserving the same sexual dignity afforded to men. As I recall, the cover hinted at essays about women uniting, about Equal Rights, about women handling both career and family, and abortion rights, newly legal—such a rush and juxtaposition of words. Fully female in a man's world, I was as excited about the magazine as I was about the cookie jar.

And how did the *Ms.* affect me? Judy Brady's satirical essay "Why I Want a Wife" may be lost on people who take it all for granted today. (The younger ones do. I am their instructor in college writing classes.) Brady, at the time a divorcee with a job and a single parent, in her essay in this premier issue was joyously and sarcastically elaborating for a male friend what a guy would be looking for and expecting in a good wife in 1972: he'd want a woman, generally, who would capitulate entirely to being the woman behind the man. Brady's own descriptions of a "woman's role" led her to the conclusion of "My God, who wouldn't want a wife!" This generic wife of the fifties, sixties, and then the seventies was devoted to her husband's every whim and need, not to mention the entire packages of needs that come with children and house, but Brady satirically pointed out that in those days the tables did not turn. The favors did not travel both ways—not for many women, at any rate. (The first *Ms.* sold out nationally in eight days. There were plenty of women who could relate.)

It's an historic essay and available on-line, but if you're young today, well, you might not get it. It might even make you, a male or female reader, mad, if you misunderstand Brady and conclude that she thinks women should be bearing the entire burden of family in support of the male head of household. A good woman, in those days, was supposed to do just that. It is such a foreign notion now that students of mine question the essay's authenticity. They just don't get it and think Brady wanted the lop-sided arrangement, or that she was a whining ingrate. She had a job and she'd had a husband. What had she done to screw that up? Complain too much? The point is that it was that way, for many, and for many it still is: a man's world. What I was reading, curled up in an uncomfortable wooden chair by the window, made my entire twenty-five years come into a sharper focus. I felt newly alive and hopeful.

There was a glimpse of my mother's pain; she had left Stanford to become a floor-scrubber and diaper washer, and eventually, a freaked-out alcoholic mother of five. One of my grandmothers had endured in silence and lots and lots of overeating; the other spent half her life in church. I understood, better now, my sister's depressions as a teenager and my own extreme sense of unfairness that society seemed to consider women second-class citizens, men's underlings. I can see my mother's laundry room when, as a high school student with no outside activities allowed (I was to come home and help with the babies and cleaning and cooking), I realized I was ironing my father's and brother's shirts while they played golf. *Ms.* verified that I wasn't alone or crazy in my awareness of this hierarchy. The males never did laundry or dishes, though my dad did cook breakfast on weekends sometimes—my mother's hangovers and all. My mother may have had choices. I'm sure she did, but she would have been mightily lacking in support for those choices. Oppression by the dominant gender and its media, repression of resistance, and depression of self-esteem seemed to be what good girls bought into, and by seventeen, I was so turned off by the rewards of being good, well, I lost interest entirely.

I didn't really know what to do with this new contact from the women at *Ms.* magazine, the uniting call to women everywhere, but I knew it was a profound day. I felt a camaraderie out there sending me signals. This glimpse of light revealed a crack in the wall: I wanted to become one of the women who would choose to speak and write and live, at least in some capacity, for themselves and their own needs. I felt like I was getting down off a shelf like my Humpty Dumpty, and I'd have to find a way to get glued back together. And it wasn't likely that a troop of the king's men would show up to help.

I certainly don't want to credit *Ms.* with my first act of speaking up and out and over the edge, but the two events were notably close in time. It was such a silly and dangerous Wild West kind of behavior. But the fact that I just didn't "take it" from him, this time—I fought back—meant a whole new world to me.

It is something I have mixed feelings about, my assault on my once best friend. If I'd hurt her badly, I would have regretted it more, I suppose. But coming from the educated middle-class, I wasn't much of a brawler and fighter. Michael had taken up with her and after a couple of months of this so-called "open relationship" (I was expected to date other guys while Michael and Kelly went out partying, dancing in Red River, or just home to her house), well, one evening in the Arroyo Seco Bar, after she'd sworn to me she was letting him go because our friendship meant too much to her—there they were, Michael and Kelly necking by the juke box. And she and I had come into the bar together to celebrate that she was letting him go so we, she and I, could be friends again.

The late afternoon sunlight, the Saturday night crowd pouring in, Taos Pueblo mesa spreading as far as the eye could see across the street, and him kissing her in public, right in front of me. He'd come in with a friend while I was dancing, and I felt like a sword had been run through my miserable heart, right where my voice had been stuck for so long: The voice

I couldn't use in college, so I'd dropped out; the voice I couldn't use when a giant had attempted to rape me, so I'd whimpered (I was luckily rescued that time); the voice I couldn't find to tell him off the first time he'd disappeared with another woman. Somehow, between the *Ms.* magazine and that sword of grief and rejection and jealousy running through me, something snapped.

And then it was her head snapping back as I assuaged my almost life-long silence with a gin and tonic glass coming down hard. The surprise factor gave me an advantage, and I was almost as surprised as she was. I'd made a conscious albeit drunken choice as she sat cross-legged; I had her by the hair. I kicked her side. I called her "bitch" (weak, but I hadn't yet had a good Shakespeare teacher) all while at least a dozen guys flew towards us to pull us apart before I killed her. It was wrong; I gladly admit that. I'd never brawled in a bar or anywhere else for that matter. But it felt good and right. And Michael was mad, me ruining his little make-out session in his fantasy world. He trotted me outside and across the narrow country road to the tiny parking lot where our boys, mine and Kelly's, were stretched out across the back seat sound asleep (different times). He threw me across the hood of her car and raised his fist and I psyched him out saying, "Go ahead, hit me big boy," hoping to God he wouldn't because I'd have a broken face if he did.

"How dare you pick on her, that poor little thing?" He showed pity for her, pitied her against the terrible, big strong me! Hah. That was pretty funny, and he let me go. Told me to walk home but I didn't. I got a ride the few blocks to our house. We'd moved to

Seco by then. And she quit him and he quit her and she left town, and I, not too much later, said a real goodbye to him.

It took a few more years, hard intentions, and good therapy to get enough pieces stuck back together so I felt worthy to exist in a healthy way: no more loser guys, no more gin (ever), no bar fights, no more poor, poor, pitiful worthlessness. And every single time I read a *Ms.*, still, I am reconfirmed. *¡Vivan las feministas!*

Merimée arrived in NM in May of 1970 and never moved back to the Coast. She lived alone with her son in and around Taos then moved to Albuquerque in 1981 to finish her college education, where she married her former beau Randy. She earned both a BA in Liberal Arts and an MA in English/Creative Writing from UNM. She and Randy have a blended family of four children and four grandchildren. After a teaching career of twenty-two years, she is currently retired and devotes her work energies to writing. She has published one book of poems, *Making Little Edens*, and her work has appeared in many anthologies and reviews. When asked how she got from the person in her memoir to the person later and now, she might reply, "One step, one day, one moment at a time. And lots of good therapy."